Study Guide and Workbook
to accompany

CULTURAL ANTHROPOLOGY
Tenth Edition

Study Guide and Workbook
to accompany

CULTURAL ANTHROPOLOGY
Tenth Edition

William A. Haviland

Prepared by

M. L. Miranda
University of Nevada, Las Vegas

WADSWORTH
™
THOMSON LEARNING

Australia • Canada • Mexico • Singapore • Spain • United Kingdom • United States

For more information about our products, contact us at:
Thomson Learning Academic Resource Center
1-800-423-0563

For permission to use material from this text, contact us by:
Phone: 1-800-730-2214
Fax: 1-800-730-2215
Web: http://www.thomsonrights.com

Asia
Thomson Learning
60 Albert Street, #15-01
Albert Complex
Singapore 189969

Australia
Nelson Thomson Learning
102 Dodds Street
South Melbourne, Victoria 3205
Australia

Canada
Nelson Thomson Learning
1120 Birchmount Road
Toronto, Ontario M1K 5G4
Canada

Europe/Middle East/Africa
Thomson Learning
Berkshire House
168-173 High Holborn
London WC1 V7AA
United Kingdom

Latin America
Thomson Learning
Seneca, 53
Colonia Polanco
11560 Mexico D.F.
Mexico

Spain
Paraninfo Thomson Learning
Calle/Magallanes, 25
28015 Madrid, Spain

Contents

Introduction
Why You Should Use the
Study Guide and Workbook

Your instructor may or may not require the use of this Study Guide and Workbook to accompany William Haviland's text, *Cultural Anthropology*, Tenth Edition. However, there are some important reasons why you might find it helpful as you begin your study of cultural anthropology.

First of all, using a study guide and workbook along with the main text for the course forces you to simply spend time with the material. You have probably found that when you think you have read an assignment for a course, often you actually can't recall much of what you read. By adding time to your reading for answering review questions, going over key vocabulary, and so on, you fix the information in your memory in a far more thorough manner. The time you spend each day on your study guide and work books will help you to spend less time "cramming" for exams later on.

Second, putting things in your own words, as our Study Guide and Workbook requires, is the best way to make the subject your own. Education researchers agree that this is a good way to ensure that simple memorization is replaced by true comprehension of information. In addition, the exercises which encourage you to grasp concepts rather than memorize words will help you on tests, in which instructors may phrase things in different ways than your textbook author does. Make the book your own; write in it, do the exercises you find useful, and skip the ones you don't. The book was prepared to help you.

Each chapter of the Study Guide and Workbook contains several sections. A *synopsis* of the chapter is followed by an outline of *what you should learn from the chapter*. Then comes a section of *key terms and names* for you to define or identify and a list of *review questions* which can be answered in a few sentences. *Fill-in-the-blank* sections will serve as further review of the material. (You can later use these pages to study for tests.) Many chapters also contain *exercises* involving constructing charts or locating cultures on maps.

To help you specifically prepare for exams, there are *multiple-choice practice questions, true/false practice questions, practice matching sets,* and *practice essays.* All of these are excellent ways of preparing for the various kinds of tests your instructor may create.

Hopefully, you will find this book to be a useful complement to William Haviland's textbook *Cultural Anthropology,* Tenth Edition. It has been revised numerous times in response to suggestions from faculty and students over the years. The best questions from previous versions of the study guide were kept.

Chapter 1
The Nature of Anthropology

Synopsis

This chapter introduces the discipline of anthropology, the study of humankind everywhere, throughout time. Anthropology seeks to produce useful generalizations about people and their behavior, to arrive at the fullest possible understanding of human diversity, and to understand those things that all human beings have in common. There are two major subfields of anthropology: physical anthropology and cultural anthropology. Physical anthropology focuses on the biological aspects of being human while cultural anthropology focuses on human beings as members of society. Because of anthropology's holistic perspective, it can contribute substantially to the resolution of human problems.

What You Should Learn from This Chapter

1. Learn how anthropology helps us to better understand ourselves:
    *   explore the impulse to find out who we are and where we came from
    *   explain how and why the discipline emerged and developed
    *   describe anthropology's relationship to the other social sciences.

2. Know the subfields of anthropology and understand their purpose and practice:
    *   physical anthropology
    *   archaeology
    *   linguistics
    *   ethnology

3. Appreciate how anthropologists conduct their research and the limits on such research.

4. Understand anthropology's relationship to the "hard sciences" and to the humanities:
    *   the hypothesis-testing framework

5. Think about some of the ethical issues that confront anthropologists today.

Key Terms

anthropology

archaeology

comparative approach

cultural anthropology

cultural deprivation

culture-bound

ethnography

ethnohistory

ethnology

forensic anthropology

holistic perspective

hypothesis

linguistic anthropology

participant observation

physical anthropology

theory

Review Questions

1. What are the four subfields of anthropology? How are they related to each other?

2. In their research, how do anthropologists attempt to be as objective and free from cultural bias as possible?

3. Distinguish between ethnology and ethnography.

4. Explain in what sense anthropology is a relatively recent product of Western civilization.

5. How does anthropology use the research of many other disciplines?

6. Why are anthropology and sociology closely allied? What sets them apart?

7. Cultural adaptation, development, and evolution are three general concerns of anthropologists. How are they interrelated?

8. Why do archaeologists excavate sites from the historical period when many documents provide information on recent culture?

9. What is the significance of "The Garbage Project?"

10. Why did archaeologists have difficulty in interpreting remains of large Mayan settlements in Central America?

11. With what aspects of language are linguists concerned?

12. Discuss why anthropology is considered the "most liberating of all sciences."

13. Distinguish between the social sciences and the humanities.

14. Discuss how human behavior and biology are inextricably intertwined. Provide examples.

15. Explain why it took so long for a systematic discipline of anthropology to appear.

16. Explain how the work of an anthropological linguist can contribute to our understanding of the human past.

17. Discuss the problems inherent in scientific anthropology.

18. Discuss the ethical problems that could arise in the process of anthropological research.

19. How do linguists aid in our study of the past?

20. Describe the role of the ethnologist, giving an example of the sort of study an ethnologist would produce.

21. What is participant-observation? What are its advantages and disadvantages when compared to other social science methods?

22. Define "ethnohistory" and discuss its contributions to historical and ethnographic understanding.

23. Why might it be advisable to do research outside one's own culture prior to studying one's own?

24. What is meant by cross-cultural comparison? What significance does it have?

25. How did anthropologist Philleo Nash affect the policies of the Roosevelt and Truman administrations?

26. What are the two key elements in the derivation of scientific laws, according to Haviland?

27. Explain the "self-correcting" nature of science, and give an example.

28. What are the limitations of the scientific approach, according to Haviland?

29. What problems are encountered when using the questionnaire for information gathering in ethnographic research?

30. How were anthropologists able to aid in the understanding of exchange relations in rural Peru?

31. What might be accomplished by research into one particular culture?

32. What distinguishes anthropology from the "hard sciences?"

33. Why must anthropologists exercise caution prior to publishing the results of their research?

34. To whom are anthropologists ultimately responsible?

35. How did Laura Nader explain her ethical position with regard to her work on the Zapotec and on U.S. energy research?

36. What is meant by a "global community?"

Fill-in-the-Blank

1. Anthropology is the study of _____ everywhere, throughout time.

2. Anthropology is one of several disciplines in the social and natural sciences that study humans. It differs from other disciplines primarily in its ability to _____ data from many sources.

3. Anthropologists recognize that human behavior has both _____ and social/cultural aspects.

4. Anthropology is divided into four branches, one of _____ anthropology and three of _____ anthropology (archaeology, linguistics, and ethnology).

5. An example of a practical application of physical anthropology is _____ anthropology, in which anthropologists testify in legal situations concerning human skeletal remains.

6. Archaeology is the study of culture based on _____ remains.

7. An in-depth description of a specific culture is called an _____.

8. Comparisons of "housework" shows that _____ spend less time on household tasks than Westerners do with all their time-saving gadgets.

9. A tentative explanation of the relation between certain phenomena (e.g., "The light failed to work because the filament was broken") is called a _____.

10. When archaeologists studied the Classic period of Maya civilization, they assumed that tropical forests occupied by people practicing _____ could not support large population clusters.

11. Ethnohistory is the study of cultures of the recent past through the analysis of _____ materials.

12. Anthropological research is just as likely to be funded by the National Science Foundation as it is by the National Endowment for the _____.

13. Whatever distinctions people may claim for themselves, they are _____ specifically, _____, and as such, they share a common ancestry with others like apes and monkeys.

14. The physical anthropologist applies all the techniques of modern _____ to achieve fuller understanding of human variation and the ways in which it relates to the different environments in which people lived.

Multiple-Choice Practice Questions

1. Anthropology is _____.
   a. the study of Western culture primarily through the analysis of its folklore.
   b. the study of humankind everywhere, throughout time.
   c. the study of nonhuman primates through behavioral analysis.
   d. the study of the species Homo sapiens by analyzing its biological but not its cultural dimensions.
   e. the analysis of humankind from the subjective perspective of one group.

2. The systematic study of humans as biological organisms.
    a. linguistic anthropology
    b. cultural ecology
    c. cultural anthropology
    d. archaeology
    e. none of the above

3. Anthropology differs from other disciplines that study humans in its ability to
    _____ data from many sources.
    a. synthesize
    b. eliminate
    c. invent
    d. falsify
    e. fabricate

4. Anthropology is traditionally divided into four branches, one of _____
    anthropology and three of _____ anthropology.
    a. cultural/physical
    b. physical/cultural
    c. archaeological/linguistic
    d. ethnological/physical
    e. biological/physical

5. As part of your job, you may study the frequency of blood types in human
    populations, watch the behavior of monkeys and apes, or dig for early hominid bones
    from East Africa. You are a/an _____.
    a. entymologist.
    b. primatologist.
    c. ethnologist.
    d. physical anthropologist.
    e. cultural anthropologist.

6. Theories about the world and reality based on the assumptions and values of one's
    own culture are _____.
    a. simplistic.
    b. irrational.
    c. culture-bound.
    d. relativistic.
    e. inductive.

7. An archaeologist might attempt to _____.
   a. study material remains to reconstruct past cultures.
   b. study present languages to reconstruct when they diverged from a parent stock.
   c. study garbage to explain contemporary behavior.
   d. all of the above
   e. *a* and *c*

8. An archaeologist studies _____.
   a. potsherds.
   b. paleoecology.
   c. genetic drift.
   d. garbage.
   e. *a, b, & d*

9. _____ is that branch of anthropology concerned with humans as biological organisms.
   a. Archaeology
   b. Cultural anthropology
   c. Ethnology
   d. Physical anthropology
   e. Paleontology

10. The focus of anthropology is on both evolution and culture as such it is able _____.
    a. to address the "nature versus nurture" question.
    b. to address certain ethical issues.
    c. to discuss the efficacy of various research methods.
    d. to address the qualitative vs quantitative methods issue.
    e. to address the political questions of the day.

11. In-depth descriptive studies of specific cultures are called _____.
    a. ethnologies.
    b. ethnobotanies.
    c. biologies.
    d. ethnographies.
    e. anthropologies.

12. The study of two or more cultures is called a/an _____.
    a. ethnology.
    b. case study.
    c. ethnography.
    d. biography.
    e. ethnohistory.

13. Anthropologists doing fieldwork typically involve themselves in many different experiences. They try to investigate not just one aspect of culture (such as the political system) but how all aspects relate to each other (for example, how the political system fits with economic institutions, religious beliefs, etc.). This approach is called the _____ perspective.
    a. holistic
    b. ethnological
    c. sociocultural
    d. sociological
    e. culture-bound

14. Ethnographic fieldwork _____.
    a. is usually associated with the study of wealthy elites.
    b. is usually associated with the study of North American society.
    c. is usually associated with the study of non-Western peoples.
    d. can be applied, with useful results, to the study of North American peoples.
    e. *c* and *d*

15. Ethnographic research on the cultural deprivation theories of the 1960s helped to demonstrate that _____.
    a. minority children are culturally deprived.
    b. cultural deprivation causes lack of achievement in minority children.
    c. the theory that minority children fail to achieve because they are culturally deprived is true.
    d. the theory that minority children fail to achieve because they are culturally deprived is a culture-bound theory.
    e. all of the above except *d*

16. Besides being interested in descriptions of particular cultures, the ethnologist is interested in _____.
    a. teaching food foragers how to use time saving gadgets.
    b. cross-cultural comparisons.
    c. descriptions of nonhuman species.
    d. promoting Western ways.
    e. providing data to various government agencies to help them suppress certain groups.

17. The goal of science is _____.
    a. to discover the universal principles that govern the workings of the visible world.
    b. to develop explanations of the world that are testable and correctable.
    c. to eliminate the need to use the imagination.
    d. all of the above
    e. *a* and *b*

18. Archaeologists studying the Classic period Mayan civilization before about 1960 made culture-bound assumptions that the Classic Maya _____.
    a. were more developed than present populations in their forms of agriculture.
    b. were food foragers.
    c. practiced the same slash-and-burn cultivation that people do today, and therefore could not have lived in large, permanent settlements.
    d. lived in large, permanent settlements based on slash-and-burn cultivation.
    e. were industrialists with space-age technology.

19. Questionnaire surveys _____.
    a. enable anthropologists to discover unexpected patterns of behavior.
    b. are never used by anthropologists.
    c. are used by anthropologists to supplement information gained by some other means.
    d. are used only by sociologists.
    e. get at real (versus ideal) patterns of behavior.

20. Ideally, on which of the following are theories in cultural anthropology based?
    a. intensive fieldwork done in a single society
    b. ethnographies from all over the world so that statements made about culture will be universally applicable
    c. worldwide questionnaire surveys
    d. intuitive thinking about society and culture based on experiences in one's own society
    e. the theories about culture formulated by the people one has studied

21. _____ refers to the study of cultures of the recent past through accounts left by explorers, missionaries, and traders, and through analysis of archival materials.
    a. Social change
    b. Ethnohistory
    c. Cross-cultural comparison
    d. Science
    e. Formulation of hypotheses

22. Anthropology studies the language of a culture, its philosophy, and its forms of art. In the process of doing research, ethnographers involve themselves intensively in the lives of those they study, trying to experience culture from their informants' points of view. In this sense, anthropology is _____.
    a. scientific.
    b. humanistic.
    c. radical.
    d. conservative.
    e. systematic.

23. In the writing and dissemination of research material the anthropologist has to consider obligations to various entities. Which of the following would *not* be one of the groups the anthropologist would be obligated to?
    a. the profession of anthropology
    b. the people who funded the study
    c. the people studied
    d. the anthropologist's parents
    e. None of the above

24. Linguistic anthropology is concerned with _____.
    a. the description of language.
    b. the history of language.
    c. how language reflects a people's understanding of the world around them.
    d. *a* and *b*
    e. *a, b,* and *c*

25. Throughout most of their history people relied on _____ and _____ for answers to questions about who they are, where they came from, and why they act as they do.
    a. myth
    b. careful observation
    c. systematic testing of data
    d. folklore
    e. *a* and *d*

26. By scientifically approaching how people live, anthropologists have learned a great deal about both human _____ and _____.
    a. frailties and strengths
    b. instincts and behavior
    c. differences and similarities
    d. insensitivity and callousness
    e. sensitivity and warmth

27. It was not until the late _____ century that a significant number of Europeans considered the behavior of others different from them to be at all relevant to an understanding of themselves.
    a. nineteenth
    b. twentieth
    c. seventeenth
    d. fourteenth
    e. eighteenth

28. As _____ of data anthropologists are well-prepared to understand the findings of other disciplines.
    a. organizers
    b. synthesizers
    c. analyzers
    d. legitimizers
    e. gatherers

29. Another name for physical anthropology is _____.
    a. primatology.
    b. evolutionary biology.
    c. bio-ecology.
    d. biological anthropology.
    e. forensic anthropology.

30. Although humans are all members of a single species, we differ from each other in some obvious and not so obvious ways. Which of the following would be ways that human differ?
    a. skin color
    b. the shape of various physical features
    c. biochemical factors
    d. susceptibility to certain diseases
    e. all of the above

31. According to Haviland, we may think of culture as the often unconscious standards by which groups of people operate. These standards are _____.
    a. genetically transmitted.
    b. biologically inherited.
    c. learned.
    d. absorbed by osmosis.
    e. none of the above

32. Another name for sociocultural anthropology is _____.
    a. ethnology.
    b. ethnography.
    c. cultural ecology.
    d. all of the above.
    e. none of the above.

33. The archaeologist is able to find out about human behavior in the past, far beyond
    the mere _____ years to which historians are limited, by their
    dependence upon written records.
    a. 20,000
    b. 10,000
    c. 5,000
    d. 7,000
    e. 8,000

34. Anthropological research techniques are applicable for which of the following
    research subjects?
    a. the study of non-western peoples
    b. the study of health care delivery systems
    c. schools
    d. corporate bureaucracies
    e. all of the above

35. _____ is/are another hallmark of anthropology.
    a. Case studies
    a. Surveys
    b. Random sampling
    c. Cross-cultural comparisons
    d. none of the above

36. In a sense, one may think of _____ as the study of alternative ways of
    doing things.
    a. participant observation
    b. ethnography
    c. ethnology
    d. case studies
    e. none of the above

37. One well known forensic anthropologist is _____.
    a. Sheilagh Brooks.
    b. Bernardo Arriaza.
    c. Jennifer Thompson.
    d. Clyde C. Snow.
    e. none of the above

38. From skeletal remains, the forensic anthropologist can **not** establish which of following?
    a. stature
    b. race
    c. sex
    d. marital status
    e. age

39. A pioneering American anthropologist who did work among the Zuni and founded the Women's Anthropological Society in 1885.
    a. Margaret Mead
    b. Ruth Benedict
    c. Martha Knack
    d. Margaret Lyneis
    e. Matilda Coxe Stevenson

40. Through the efforts of _____ many of the great anthropology museums were established.
    a. Franz Boas
    b. Bronislaw Malinowski
    c. John Wesley Powell
    d. Leslie White
    e. Fredric Ward Putnam

41. He established the Bureau of American Ethnology in 1879.
    a. Robert Kroeber
    b. George Peter Murdock
    c. John Wesley Powell
    d. Sean Conlin
    e. Clyde Wood

42. Modern cross cultural studies in anthropology derive from efforts of this pioneering anthropologist to develop a rigorous methodology.
    a. George Peter Murdock
    b. John Wesley Powell
    c. Sir Edward B. Tylor
    d. Peggy Reeves Sanday
    e. Laura Nader

43. Which of the following services is **not** one that forensic anthropologists are routinely called upon by the police and other authorities to do?
    a. identify potential archaeological sites
    b. identify the remains of murder victims
    c. identify missing persons
    d. identify people who have died in disasters
    e. identify victims of genocide

44. Among the skeletal remains studied by forensic anthropologist Clyde Snow are the remains of _____.
    a. Julius Caesar.
    b. General George A. Custer.
    c. Adolf Hitler.
    d. Josef Mengele.
    e. *b* and *d*

45. This woman anthropologist was hired by the Bureau of American Ethnology in 1888, making her one of the first women in the U.S. to receive a full-time position in science.
    a. Margaret Mead
    b. Ruth Benedict
    c. Matilda Coxe Stevenson
    d. Laura Nader
    e. Martha Knack

46. _____ and his students made anthropology courses a common part of college and university curricula.
    a. John Wesley Powell
    b. Fredric Ward Putnam
    c. Bronislaw Malinowski
    d. Claude Levi-Strauss
    e. Franz Boas

47. His classification of Indian languages north of Mexico is still consulted by scholars today.
    a. Franz Boas
    b. Noam Chomsky
    c. Gary Palmer
    d. John Wesley Powell
    e. George Urioste

48. This woman anthropologist examined a sample of 156 societies drawn from the Human Relations Area File (HRAF) in an attempt to answer such questions as: Why, and under what circumstances, do men dominate women? Why do women play a more dominant role in some societies than others?
    a. Laura Nader
    b. Peggy Reeves Sanday
    c. A. B. Weiner
    d. Ruth Benedict
    e. Margaret Mead

49. Luis Vivanco's fieldwork, as depicted in the Original Study, took place in
    _____.
    a. rural Guatemala.
    b. the slums of Mexico City.
    c. urban Panama.
    d. rural Costa Rica.
    e. downtown Managua.

50. As discussed in the Original Study, Luis Vivanco's Costa Rican research focused on the cultural dynamics of which of the following?
    a. ecotourism
    b. marketing practices
    c. nature conservation
    d. shamanism
    e. *a* and *c*

Answers to multiple-choice practice questions

1. b	14. e	27. e	40. a
2. e	15. d	28. b	41. c
3. a	16. b	29. d	42. a
4. b	17. e	30. e	43. a
5. d	18. c	31. c	44. e
6. c	19. c	32. a	45. c
7. e	20. b	33. c	46. e
8. e	21. b	34. e	47. d
9. d	22. b	35. d	48. b
10. a	23. d	36. c	49. d
11. d	24. e	37. d	50. e
12. a	25. e	38. d	
13. a	26. c	39. e	

True/False Practice Questions

1. _____ Culture is preserved and transmitted by language and observation.

2. _____ While ethnography is the in-depth study of a single culture, ethnology is the comparative study of culture.

3. _____ Ethnographic fieldwork is never done in Western societies.

4. _____ Anthropology can best be defined as the cross-cultural study of social behavior.

5. _____ Forensic anthropologists are particularly interested in the use of anthropological information for the purpose of debate, oratory and rhetorical criticism.

6. _____ As pointed out in the Original Study, the national currency of Costa Rica is the peso.

7. _____ A forensic anthropologist can even tell from skeletal remains whether the deceased was right or left handed.

8. _____ What a forensic anthropologist cannot tell from skeletal remains are details of an individual's health and nutritional history.

9. _____ Besides providing factual accounts of the fate of victims who had disappeared (*desparecidos*) to their surviving kin, Snow's work helped convict several Argentine military officers of kidnaping, torture, and murder.

10. _____ All cases of forensic anthropologists involve the abuse of police powers, and evidence provided by them is often ancillary to bringing the guilty party to justice.

11. _____ Franz Boas was the first to teach anthropology in the United States.

12. _____ Since the subject matter of anthropology is vast, a single anthropologist is personally able to investigate everything that has to do with people.

13. _____ Anthropologists know that if formulated correctly their theories will be completely beyond challenge.

14. _____ Archaeologists are cultural anthropologists.

15. _____ Ethnologists study languages throughout time to determine how they have changed.

16. _____ Anthropologists think of their findings as something apart from those of other social scientists.

17. _____ The subdisciplines of physical and cultural anthropology are closely related, since we cannot understand what people do unless we know what people are.

18. _____ Physical anthropologists just study fossil skulls, they would not be interested in studying the recently deceased.

19. _____ According to anthropological research, in North American society the ever-increasing amount of household appliance consumer goods has in fact resulted in a steady reduction in household work, with a consequent increase in leisure time.

20. _____ In a sense, one may think of ethnology as the study of alternative ways of doing things.

Answers to true/false practice questions

1. T	6. F	11. F	16. F
2. T	7. T	12. F	17. T
3. F	8. F	13. F	18. F
4. F	9. T	14. T	19. F
5. F	10. F	15. F	20. T

Practice Matching

Match the disciplines/concepts with their correct description.

1. _____Anthropology

2. _____Physical anthropology

3. _____Cultural anthropology

4. _____Forensic anthropology

5. _____Culture-bound

6. _____Archaeology

a. Field of applied physical anthropology that specializes in the identification of human skeletal remains for legal purposes.

b. The systematic study of humans as biological organisms.

c. The study of humankind, in all times and places.

d. The branch of anthropology that focuses on human behavior.

e. The study of material remains, usually from the past, to describe and explain human behavior.

f. Theories about the world and reality based on the assumptions and values of one's own culture.

Answers to practice matching questions

1. c	3. d	5. f
2. b	4. a	6. e

Practice Essays

1. Illustrate the usefulness of ethnographic fieldwork in North American society by discussing research on the theory of cultural deprivation among minority children.

2. Discuss the characteristics of participant-observation and how this method contributes to ethnographic understanding. How is this method characteristically different from other methods of social science research?

3. Describe how anthropology is, at the same time, a social/behavioral science, a natural science, and one of the humanities.

4. It was stated that it has been the office of other social sciences is to reassure; while the role of anthropology is to unsettle. Explain what is meant by this.

5. According to the professional code of ethics of the American Anthropological Association, an anthropologist's primary responsibility is to the people he or she studies. Discuss the ethical issues that might arise where there is a conflict of interest between the scholar's commitment to the "truth" and his or her commitment to people.

6. Haviland asserts that anthropology is a kind of testing ground for the cross-cultural validity of disciplines like sociology, psychology, and economics, saying that it is to these disciplines what the laboratory is to physics and chemistry. What theory in another social science discipline can you think of that could usefully be tested cross-culturally?

7. The original study, "Encountering Environmentalism in Rural Costa Rica," illustrates several important factors anyone about to conduct anthropological research should know. What are those factors?

8. Your textbook provides a rather lengthy discussion of the difficulties that arise in the application of the scientific approach in anthropology. What are the difficulties that arise when applying the scientific approach in anthropology?

9. How can a cultural practice affect human biology? Explain.

10. Who is Clyde Snow? Describe his work

Chapter 2
The Nature of Culture

Synopsis

In Chapter 2 the author considers the concept of culture, which underlies the anthropological enterprise. He proposes possible avenues for the definition of culture and describes how anthropologists attempt to study culture in the field. Finally, he raises questions as to whether it is possible for anthropologists to evaluate and compare cultures.

What You Should Learn from This Chapter

1. Understand what culture is.

2. Know how culture is transmitted along generations.

3. Know how anthropologists conduct research into cultures.

4. Understand how culture functions in society.

5. Understand the relationship between culture and adaptation.

Key Terms and Names

A.R. Radcliffe-Brown

adaptation

Bronislaw Malinowski

cultural relativism

culture

enculturation

ethnocentrism

gender

integration

Leslie White

pluralistic societies

social structure

society

structural-functionalism

subcultures

symbol

Review Questions

1. What are four characteristics of culture, according to Haviland?

2. Distinguish between "culture" and "society." Do they always go together?

3. Distinguish between sex and gender.

4. Give an example of a pluralistic society, and consider what factors seem to allow the larger culture to tolerate subcultural variation.

5. How is culture passed on?

6. What is meant by the "integration" of various aspects of culture? Give an example.

7. How was anthropology able to contribute to the architectural problems of the Apache Indians?

8. What are three ways in which anthropologists should obtain data in another culture, according to the text?

9. How did Malinowski define the "needs" to be fulfilled by all cultures?

10. What did Annette Weiner find out about Trobriand women?

11. What five functions must a culture serve, according to your text?

12. What changes have recently impacted many pastoralists in sub-Saharan Africa?

13. In what ways must a balance be struck between society and the individuals who comprise it?

14. How can the large-scale sacrifices of the Aztec be explained?

15. Distinguish between ethnocentrism and cultural relativism.

16. According to Walter Goldschmidt, what aspects of society indicate how well the physical and psychological needs of its people are being met?

17. What was E.B. Tylor's original definition of culture in 1871? (This is a classic definition in anthropology, so it would be worthwhile to become familiar with it).

18. Approximately how old is human culture?

Fill-in-the-Blank

1. The culture concept was first developed in the _____ century.

2. Haviland defines culture as "a set of _____ shared by members of a society that when acted upon by the members of a society, produce behavior that falls withing a range of variance the members consider proper and acceptable."

3. When groups function within a society with their own distinctive standards of behavior, we speak of _____ variation.

4. Enculturation refers to the process through which culture is transmitted from one _____ to the next.

5. According to anthropologist _____, all human behavior originates in the use of symbols.

6. Radcliffe-Brown was the originator of a school of thought known as _____.

7. In Kapauku culture, gardens of _____ supply most of the food, but it is through breeding pigs that a man achieves political power.

8. There is a difference between what people say the rules are and actual behavior; that is, the anthropologist must distinguish between the _____ and the real.

9. Inheritance among the Trobrianders is carried through the _____ line.

10. Most organisms adapt by acquiring changes in their _____.

11. Pastoral nomadic people in Africa south of the _____ have survived droughts because of their mobility.

12. The members of all societies consider their own culture to be the best; thus all people can be said to be _____.

13. Anthropology tries to promote cultural _____, or the idea that a culture must be evaluated according to its own standards.

Exercise

Briefly identify the cultures listed below and locate them on the world map.

1. Amish

3. Trobrianders

2. Kapauku Papuans

4. Apache

Multiple-Choice Practice Questions

1. The contemporary definition of culture has changed from the meaning given to it during the nineteenth century. Today,
   a. culture is seen as values and beliefs that lie behind behavior rather than as actual behavior.
   b. culture is seen as real rather than as ideal.
   c. the term "culture" has been replaced by the term "society."
   d. culture is defined as objects rather than ideas.
   e. the term "culture" is not used.

2. One way to determine if people share the same culture is to observe whether they _____.
   a. are dependent on each other for survival.
   b. are able to interpret and predict each other's actions.
   c. live in the same territory.
   d. behave in an identical manner.
   e. all of the above.

3. Which of the following statements about society and culture is **incorrect**?
   a. Culture can exist without a society.
   b. A society can exist without culture.
   c. Ants and bees have societies but no culture.
   d. A culture is shared by the members of a society.
   e. Although members of a society may share a culture, their behavior is not uniform.

4. Every culture teaches its members that there are differences between people based on sex, age, occupation, class, and ethnic group. People learn to predict the behavior of people playing different roles from their own. This means that _____.
   a. culture is shared even though everyone is not the same.
   b. everyone plays the same role.
   c. all cultures identify the same roles.
   d. all cultures require that their participants play different roles, even though that means that no one can predict the behavior of others.
   e. everyone plays the same role throughout his or her life.

5. The cultural definitions of what it means to be a male or female today _____.
   a. are determined by biological differences.
   b. are independent of biological differences.
   c. stem from biological differences that today are relatively insignificant.
   d. developed about 60 million years ago.
   e. have no relationship to sex.

6. When groups function within a society with their own distinctive standards of behavior, we speak of _____.
   a. subcultural variation.
   b. social structure.
   c. gender differences.
   d. cultural materialism.
   e. ethnocentrism.

7. The Amish may be used as an example of a/an _____.
   a. pluralistic society.
   b. subculture.
   c. integrated society.
   d. world culture.
   e. complex society.

8. The process by which culture is transmitted from one generation to the next is _____.
   a. enculturation.
   b. pluralism.
   c. adaptation.
   d. cultural relativism.
   e. subcultural variation.

9. Which of the following statements is **incorrect**?
   a. All culture is learned.
   b. All learned behavior is cultural.
   c. Culture is humankind's "social heredity."
   d. Culture is not biologically inherited.
   e. The process whereby culture is transmitted from one generation to the next is called enculturation.

10. The most important symbolic aspect of culture is _____.
    a. art.
    b. language.
    c. religion.
    d. money.
    e. politics.

11. Among the Kapauku Papuans of New Guinea, the fact that an attempt to eliminate warfare (Which would create a balanced sex ratio) would affect the practice of polygyny, which would affect the economy (since women raise pigs, and the more wives a man has the more pigs he can keep), shows that culture is

    _____.
    a. materialistic.
    b. relative.
    c. pluralistic.
    d. integrated.
    e. enculturated.

12. An anthropologist develops a concept of culture by considering which of the following sources of data from the field?
    a. what people say they ought to do
    b. how people think they are behaving in accordance with these rules
    c. what people actually do
    d. all of the above
    e. none of the above

13. When Annette Weiner went to the Trobriand Islands sixty years after Malinowski had been there, she found that _____.
    a. the culture had changed so much that it was almost unrecognizable.
    b. Malinowski's views of wealth, political power, and descent were primarily from the male's point of view.
    c. Malinowski had attributed power to women that did not exist.
    d. only women were significant producers of wealth.
    e. women played no role in producing wealth.

14. The process by which organisms adjust beneficially to their environment, or the characteristics by which they overcome hazards and gain access to the resources they need to survive, is called _____.
    a. culture.
    b. biology.
    c. social structure.
    d. integration.
    e. adaptation.

15. Behavior can be adaptive in the short run but maladaptive in the long run. In the Central Valley in California, vast irrigation projects have created a garden, but salts and chemicals accumulating in the soil will eventually create another desert. This same process occurred in _____.
    a. Mexico.
    b. Morocco.
    c. ancient Mesopotamia.
    d. Great Britain.
    e. the Yellow River valley of China.

16. A culture must satisfy basic needs such as _____.
    a. the distribution of necessary goods and services.
    b. biological continuity through reproduction and enculturation of functioning adults.
    c. maintenance of order within a society and between a society and outsiders.
    d. motivation to survive.
    e. all of the above

17. According to Leslie White, which of the following is a symbol?
    a. a painting
    b. a novel
    c. walking across an intersection
    d. brushing your teeth
    e. all of the above

18. _____ refers to the position that because cultures are unique, each one should be evaluated according to its own standards and values.
    a. Ethnocentrism
    b. Cultural relativism
    c. Cultural materialism
    d. Adaptation
    e. Pluralism

19. Goldschmidt suggests that it is possible to decide which cultures are more successful than others by looking at which ones _____.
    a. survive.
    b. last the longest.
    c. satisfy the physical and cultural needs of the people.
    d. support the most people.
    e. are the least emotional.

20. When anthropologist _____ observed that all human behavior originates in the use of symbols, he expressed an opinion shared by all anthropologists.
    a. Alfred Kroeber
    b. E.E. Evans-Pritchard
    c. Francis Shu
    d. A.F.C. Wallace
    e. Leslie White

21. A mountain people of western New Guinea studied in 1955 by the North American anthropologist Leo Pospisil.
    a. !Kung San
    b. Kaluli
    c. Basseri
    d. Kapauku
    e. Azande

22. We now know that any culture that is functioning adequately regards itself as the best, a view reflecting a phenomenon known as _____.
    a. cultural relativism.
    b. egoism.
    c. nationalistic.
    d. ethnocentrism.
    e. individualism.

23. The idea that one must suspend judgement on other peoples' practices in order to understand them in their own cultural terms is called _____.
    a. structuralism.
    b. functionalism.
    c. structural functionalism.
    d. cultural relativism.
    e. relative culturalism.

24. In regards to the concept of cultural relativism, anthropologist _____ emphasized that "...one does not avoid making judgements, but rather postpones them in order to make informed judgements later."
    a. David Maybury-Lewis
    b. Daniel Day-Lewis
    c. Francis L.K. Shu
    d. E.E. Evans-Pritchard
    e. A.F.C. Wallace

25. As a result of _____ work, in 1981, the Apaches were able to move into houses that had been designed with *their* participation, for *their* specific needs.
    a. Walter Goldschmidt's
    b. George Esber's
    c. David Maybury-Lewis's
    d. Bronislaw Kasper Malinowski's
    e. Margaret Mead's

26. The British anthropologist _____ was the originator of what has come to be known as the structural-functionalist school of thought.
    a. Claude Levi-Strauss
    b. George Simmel
    c. A.R. Radcliffe-Brown
    d. Leslie A. White
    e. Ruth Benedict

27. _____ was a major theoretician in North American anthropology who saw culture as consisting of three essential components, which he referred to as techno-economic, the social, and the ideological.
    a. A.R. Radcliffe-Brown
    b. Leslie A. White
    c. Leopold Pospisil
    d. A.B. Weiner
    e. William Jankowiak

28. To insure survival of a group of people, a culture must do which of the following?
    a. satisfy the basic needs of those who live by its rules
    b. provide for its own continuity
    c. provide an orderly existence for members of a society
    d. have the capacity to change
    e. all of the above

29. To answer such questions as: why do particular customs arise in the first place, and how do cultures change? _____ approaches are necessary.
    a. Structural
    b. Functional
    c. Historical
    d. Mechanical
    e. Structural-functional

30. In 1871, _____ defined culture as "that complex whole which includes knowledge, belief, art, law, morals, custom and any other capabilities and habits acquired by man as a member of society.
    a. A.L. Kroeber
    b. Clyde Kluckhohn
    c. Edward Burnett Taylor
    d. Karl Marx
    e. Margaret Mead

31. Which of the following is **not** a characteristic of society?
    a. A group of people who share a common homeland.
    b. A group of people who are dependent on each other for survival.
    c. A group of people who share a culture.
    d. A group of people who share a common identity.
    e. All of the above are characteristic of a society.

32. To survive, a culture must _____.
    a. satisfy the basic needs of those who live by its rules.
    b. provide for its own continuity.
    c. furnish an orderly existence for the members of its society.
    d. strike a balance between the self-interests of individuals and the needs of society as a whole.
    e. all of the above

33. Gender differences are as old as human culture, or about _____ years.
    a. 5 million
    b. 2.5 million
    c. 100,000
    d. 250,000
    e. 1 million

34. The thesis that one must suspend judgment on other peoples' practices to understand them in their own cultural terms.
    a. Ethnocentrism
    b. Separatism
    c. Social relativism
    d. Socialism
    e. Cultural relativism

35. The job of anthropologists is to abstract a set of rules from what they observe to explain the social behavior of a people. To arrive at a realistic description of a culture free from personal and cultural biases, anthropologists must _____.
    a. based on the anthropologists' culture, make judgements on other peoples' practices to understand them.
    b. examine a people's notion of the way their society ought to function.
    c. determine how a people think they behave.
    d. compare how people think they ought to behave with how they actually behave.
    e. *b, c,* and *d*

36. Although citizens of the United States are fond of boasting that theirs is the finest health care system in the world, they are merely reflecting _____ of their own culture.
    a. nationalism
    b. eclecticism
    c. ethnocentrism
    d. relativism
    e. euphemism

37. Through culture, the human species has secured not just its survival but its expansion. Which of the following would be examples of human expansion?
    a. settlements in the Arctic region
    b. flights to the moon
    c. settlements in the Sahara Desert
    d. the exploration of space
    e. all of the above

Answers to multiple-choice practice questions

1. a	11. d	21. d	31. e
2. b	12. d	22. d	32. e
3. a	13. b	23. d	33. b
4. a	14. e	24. a	34. e
5. c	15. c	25. b	35. e
6. a	16. e	26. c	36. c
7. b	17. e	27. b	37. e
8. a	18. b	28. e	
9. b	19. c	29. c	
10. b	20. e	30. c	

True/False Practice Questions

1. _____ To say that culture is shared means that all members of a society behave in the same way.

2. _____ A pluralistic society always has subcultural variation, but not every society with subcultural variation is pluralistic.

3. _____ A larger culture is more likely to tolerate a subculture if their values and physical appearances are similar.

4. _____ Cattle herding is the mainstay around which all of Kapauku Papuan society revolves.

5. _____ A modern definition of culture emphasizes the values, beliefs, and rules that lie behind behavior rather than the actual observable behavior itself.

6. _____ Gender differences were more extreme among food foragers than among late nineteenth and early twentieth century Westerners.

7. _____ Annette Weiner agrees that ethnographic writing can never be more than a fictional account.

8. _____ There are some societies that have no regulation of sex whatsoever.

9. _____ There can be no culture without a society.

10. _____ Ants and bees instinctively cooperate in a manner that clearly indicates a degree of social organization, therefore they have culture.

11. _____ Though one's sex is culturally determined, one's sexual identity or gender is biologically constructed.

12. _____ The degree of tolerance accorded the Amish is due in part to the fact that they are "white" Europeans.

13. _____ So-called racial characteristics represent biological adaptations to climate and have nothing to do with differences in intelligence or cultural superiority.

14. _____ Learned behavior is exhibited to one degree or another by most, if not all, mammals.

15. _____ If a society is to survive it must succeed in balancing the self-interest of its members against the demands of the society as a whole.

16. _____ Numerous studies by a variety of social scientists have clearly shown that the death penalty does deter violent crime in the United States.

17. _____ Cross cultural studies show that homicide rates mostly decline after the death penalty is abolished.

18. _____ Universally, individuals are regarded as adults when they reach the age of eighteen.

19. _____ People maintain cultures to deal with problems or matters that concern them.

20. _____ A culture must have the capacity to change so it can adapt to altered perceptions of existing circumstances.

21. _____ Cultures are biologically inherited, rather than learned.

22. _____ Humans do everything because it is adaptive to a particular environment.

23. _____ What is adaptive in one context may be seriously maladaptive in another.

Answers to true/false practice questions

1. F	7. F	13. T	19. T
2. T	8. F	14. T	20. T
3. T	9. T	15. T	21. F
4. F	10. F	16. F	22. F
5. T	11. F	17. T	23. T
6. F	12. T	18. F	

Practice Matching

Match the culture with its description.

1. ____Amish
2. ____Trobrianders
3. ____Kapauku Papuans
4. ____Aztec
5. ____Apache

a. A Native American people with distinct architectural needs.
b. A Pacific Island people studied by both Malinowski and Weiner.
c. A pacifist agrarian subculture of the U.S.
d. A New Guinea people who breed pigs.
e. A civilization in Mexico that engaged in large-scale sacrifices.

Answers to practice matching

1. c   2. b   3. d   4. e   5. a

Practice Essays

1. Using the Amish as an example of subcultural variation, discuss some of the factors that seem to determine whether or not subcultural variation is tolerated by the larger culture. Compare the Amish to another group that is less well-tolerated.

2. Distinguish between the concepts of culture and society.

3. Discuss the distinction between sex and gender and explain why this distinction is important.

4. Discuss the interrelatedness of the various parts of Kapauku culture. Use examples.

5. Because of the male bias of his European culture, Bronislaw Malinowski's pioneering study of the Trobriand Islanders missed many important factors. Discuss the factors that were overlooked due to male bias.

6. Provide examples to support the statement, "What is adaptive in one context may be seriously maladaptive in another."

7. Using the example of the Kapauku Papuans, explain the idea that culture is integrated.

8. Anthropologist James Peacock wrote a book called *The Anthropological Lens* in which he compared culture to a lens or glass through which people experience the world. The anthropologist, then, is like an oculist who hopes to find the "formula" of each kind of lens, acquiring a kind of stereoscopy, or depth perception, by being able to perceive things through multiple lenses. How is culture like a lens? What are the limitations of this metaphor for understanding culture and anthropology?

9. Are animals other than humans capable of culture?

10. Explain why people maintain cultures?

Chapter 3
The Beginnings of
Human Culture

Synopsis

Culture evolved as the primary adaptation of our species over millions of year. In this chapter Haviland traces the intertwining of biological and cultural evolution through the history of our fossil ancestors, looking at major milestones like the development of stone tools, the first use of fire, the rise of cooperative hunting, and language as a means of communication.

What You Should Learn from This Chapter

1. Understand that culture is our species' major mode of adaptation.

2. Know the major fossil ancestors of our species and approximately where and when they lived.

3. Understand the biological changes that led to the current physical structure of our species.

4. Know what the major milestones in the development of culture were, and approximately where and when they occurred.

5. Understand how the study of human evolution complements and enhances the study of the diversity of cultures today.

Key Terms and Names

Ardipithecus

Australopithecus

hominine

Homo erectus

Homo habilis

Homo sapiens

Jane Goodall

Mousterian tools

natural selection

Neandertals

Oldowan tools

Paleolithic

primate order

Upper Paleolithic

Review Questions

1. To what biological order do humans belong? What other kinds of animals belong to this order?

2. Describe the environment to which early primates adapted through natural selection.

3. What are the distinguishing features of the primates?

4. In what ways can apes adapt to their environment through learning?

5. Why is dentition important to the study of human evolution?

6. Under what conditions might bipedalism have emerged?

7. What features of *Australopithecus* were more humanlike, and what features were more apelike?

8. What are the fossil species into which *Australopithecus* is divided? Identify each.

9. What was the "protein problem" faced by evolving primates? How was it resolved?

10. When and where did the first stone tools appear? What were they like?

11. How did the appearance of stone tools relate to changes in brain size, teeth, and diet?

12. How did the different roles played by males and females in the search for food affect selection for intelligence in early *Homo*?

13. What was the geographical distribution of *Homo erectus*? What were its physical characteristics?

14. What was the impact of the use of fire on our fossil ancestors?

15. What other cultural developments took place during *Homo erectus* times?

16. What is the difference between a hominine and a hominoid?

17. What is the role played by grooming in primate social order?

18. When did *Homo sapiens* first appear? What were its characteristics?

19. What is the "out of Africa" hypothesis? What is the evidence for and against it?

20. What was the tool-making tradition of the Neandertals?

21. In what other ways did culture develop in Neandertal times?

22. What were the major cultural developments of the Upper Paleolithic?

Fill-in-the-Blank

1. Humans belong to the _____ Order, along with lemurs, indriids, lorises, tarsiers, monkeys, and apes.

2. Primates have fewer and less _____ teeth in comparison to the ancestral animals from which they evolved.

3. The senses that are highly developed in primates are _____, touch, and smell.

4. The tree-dwelling environment to which early primates adapted is called an _____ habitat.

5. The depth perception characteristic of primates stems from their _____ vision.

6. Instead of claws, most primates have _____.

7. Primate brains are large, especially the _____ hemispheres.

8. A behavior of primates that encourages social bonding is _____.

9. Jane Goodall carried out a long-term study of chimpanzees in _____.

10. The first hominine to walk fully upright was _____.

11. Walking on two legs is called _____.

12. A new find that may represent the earliest form of *Australopithecus* is _____.

13. The earliest stone tools are about _____ million years old.

14. It was *Homo* _____ who made Oldowan tools.

15. *Homo erectus* spread beyond Africa to _____.

16. Neandertal tool-making traditions are called _____.

17. The _____ hypothesis suggests that all modern humans are derived from a single population of archaic *H. sapiens*.

18. Upper Paleolithic peoples spread into two new geographic areas: _____ and _____.

Exercises

I. Map

On the world map below, mark the approximate ranges of the following fossil forms (make a key so that you can use this to study from).

   a. *Ardipithecus*
   b. *Australopithecus*
   c. *Homo habilis*
   d. *Homo erectus*
   e. *Homo sapiens*

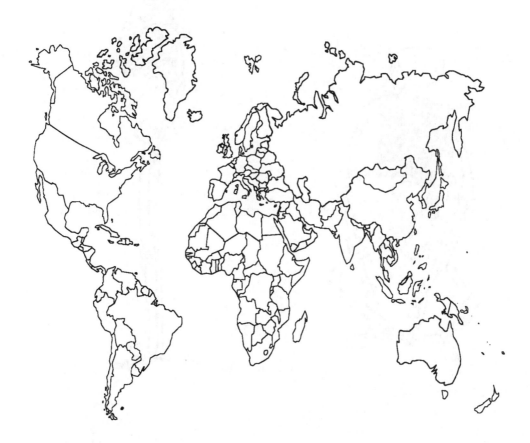

II. Comparative Skeletal Structure

Below are skeletons of a chimpanzee and a modern human being. Discuss the major
anatomical differences between them, pointing out what selective pressures might be
responsible. (Using colors to mark similar structures may help make this clearer for
review purposes.)

III. Complete the following chart to use as a study aid in reviewing human evolution.

Fossil Form	Dates	Range	Characteristics	Cultural Developments
Ardipithecus				
Australopithecus				
Homo habilis				
Homo erectus				
Neandertals				
Upper Paleolithic *Homo sapiens*				

Multiple-Choice Practice Questions

1. The primate order includes which of the following types of animals?
   a. tarsiers
   b. lorises
   c. lemurs
   d. apes
   e. all of the above

2. Which of the following characteristics distinguishes primates from other animals?
   a. a large complex brain in which the area devoted to smell is quite large
   b. the development of more teeth of a highly specialized nature
   c. increased visual capacity because of stereoscopic and color vision
   d. the development of a specific breeding season and increased number of offspring
   e. all of the above

3. The Indo-European language family is subdivided into some 11 subgroups, which reflect the fact that there has been a _____ year or more of linguistic divergence.
   a. 1,000
   b. 12,000
   c. 4,000
   d. 6,500
   e. 6,000

4. The transition to bipedalism probably occurred in a context where primates spent a lot of time in the trees but ventured out periodically onto the open savanna to exploit the food resources there. This transition occurred because bipedalism conferred the advantage of _____.
   a. being able to climb trees more effectively.
   b. being able to run faster on the ground.
   c. freeing the hands for a variety of purposes.
   d. being able to see greater distances.
   e. an improved sense of smell.

5. *Australopithecus* was more like an ape than a human in its _____.
   a. teeth.
   b. jaws.
   c. brain-body ratio.
   d. posture and form of locomotion.
   e. all of the above

6. The earliest known tool tradition _____.
   a. is called Oldowan.
   b. begins about 2 million years ago.
   c. marks the beginning of the Paleolithic.
   d. marks the end of the Paleolithic.
   e. *a, b,* and *c*

7. Which form had a geographic range of Africa, Southeast Asia, Europe, and China?
   a. *Australopithecus*
   b. *Ardipithecus*
   c. *Homo erectus*
   d. *Homo habilis*
   e. all of the above

8. This population developed an extensive art and decorative tradition.
   a. *Homo habilis*
   b. *Homo erectus*
   c. Neandertal
   d. Upper Paleolithic peoples
   e. fully modern *Homo sapiens*

9. Jane Goodall is highly respected for her work with _____.
   a. chimpanzees.
   b. gorillas.
   c. orangutans.
   d. macaques.
   e. lorises.

10. A pioneer in the study of primate behavior.
    a. Ruth Benedict
    b. Margaret Mead
    c. Jane Goodall
    d. Benjamin Beck
    e. Ashley Montagu

11. Both the fossil data and comparisons of DNA and other biochemical measures suggest that the _____ is the most conservative, or primitive of the great apes.
    a. gorilla
    b. chimpanzee
    c. macaque
    d. orangutan
    e. tarsier

12. At the genetic level, humans and chimpanzees are at least _____ percent identical.
    a. 100
    b. 98.5
    c. 75.1
    d. 50.25
    e. 25.4

13. In captivity, orangutans have been known to do which of the following?
    a. speak in brief unintelligible sentences
    b. use one tool to make another
    c. recognize themselves in mirrors
    d. manipulate objects
    e. *b, c,* and *d*

14. This woman primatologist studied gorillas.
    a. Birute Galdikas
    b. Diane Fossey
    c. Jane Goodall
    d. Laura Nader
    e. Mary Leakey

15. In July of 1960 Jane Goodall arrived at the Gombe Chimpanzee Reserve, on the shores of Lake Tanganyika in _____.
    a. Zaire.
    b. Kenya.
    c. Mozambique.
    d. Tanzania.
    e. Uganda.

16. Present evidence suggest that humans evolved from small, apelike primates that lived between _____ and _____ million years ago.
    a. 20/10
    b. 40/15
    c. 35/5
    d. 15/8
    e. 10/7

17. The process of _____ favors not just the survival of well-adapted individuals, but the propagation of their genetic traits.
    a. acculturation
    b. assimilation
    c. select breeding
    d. natural selection
    e. biological convergence

18. The behavior of early hominines probably was comparable to which of the following modern-day primates?
    a. baboons
    b. chimpanzees
    c. macaques
    d. bonobos
    e. *b* and *d*

19. The young chimp learns how to interact with others, and even manipulate them for his or her own benefit by which of the following techniques?
    a. social facilitation
    b. observation
    c. imitation
    d. practice
    e. all of the above

20. Which of the following items could be part of the diet of chimps and bonobos?
    a. small animals
    b. fruits
    c. plants other than fruits
    d. medium-sized animals
    e. all of the above

21. For hominines _____ was an important adaptive feature in the savanna environment.
    a. the prehensile thumb
    b. the prehensile tail
    c. the ability to swim
    d. bipedalism
    e. the ability to fly

22. It is thought that *H. erectus'* move into Europe may have involved the use of watercraft, as the earliest sites are in Italy and Spain. Convincing evidence for the use of watercraft as early as _____ years ago comes from _____.
    a. 800,000/Indonesia.
    b. 1,000,000/Greece.
    c. 500,000/Turkey.
    d. 100,000/England.
    e. 250,000/Siberia.

23. If one professes the belief that the fossil evidence suggests that local populations in Africa, eastern and southern Asia, and possibly Europe, together made the transition from *Homo erectus* to modern *Homo sapiens*, that person is espousing the _____ hypothesis.
    a. "out of Africa"
    b. "Eve"
    c. "multiregional"
    d. "out of Asia"
    e. "out of Siberia"

24. _____ exploits the evolution of novel functions in microbes to clean up toxic waste.
    a. Biosynthesis
    b. Bioremediation
    c. Bioradiation
    d. Biotechnology
    e. Biomedical instrumentation

25. The evolutionary mechanism by which individuals with characteristics best suited to a particular environment survive and reproduce with greater frequency than those without them.
    a. selective bias
    b. adaptation
    c. reproductive selection
    d. natural selection
    e. phylogyny

26. Human culture, as we know it, came into existence _____ years ago.
    a. 2.5 million
    b. 1.5 million
    c. 10 million
    d. 5 million
    e. 100 million

27. Which of the following would be among the cognitive skills possessed by the orangutan Chantek?
    a. had comprehension of spoken English
    b. could tell lies
    c. could refer to things or events not present
    d. was capable of deception
    e. all of the above

28. The earliest species of the genus Homo.
    a. *Homo erectus*
    b. *Neanderthal*
    c. *Homo sapiens*
    d. *Homo habilis*
    e. *Australopithecus afarensis*

29. The representative group of archaic *Homo sapiens* living in Europe, the Middle East, and south central Asia from about 120,000 years ago to about 35,000 years ago.
    a. *Neanderthal*
    b. *Homo erectus*
    c. *Australopithecus afarensis*
    d. *Homo habilis*
    e. *Ardipithecus ramidus*

30. A toolmaking tradition of the Neanderthals and their contemporaries of Europe, southwest Asia, and North Africa.
    a. Oldowan
    b. Upper Paleolithic
    c. Mousterian
    d. Acheulean
    e. Levalloisian

31. All monkeys, apes, and chimpanzees have common characteristics. Identify those characteristics from the list below.
    a. lack the ability to make tools
    b. can use tools
    c. live in social groups
    d. communicate through visual and vocal signals
    e. all but *a*

32. Hunting among _____ frequently involves teamwork to trap and kill prey.
    a. baboons
    b. chimpanzees
    c. orangutans
    d. gorillas
    e. macaques

Answers to multiple-choice practice questions

1. e	9. a	17. d	25. d
2. c	10. c	18. e	26. a
3. d	11. d	19. e	27. e
4. c	12. b	20. e	28. d
5. c	13. e	21. d	29. a
6. e	14. b	22. a	30. c
7. c	15. d	23. c	31. e
8. d	16. d	24. b	32. b

True/False Practice Questions

1. _____ The environment selected for the distinctive characteristics of the primate order was arboreal.

2. _____ Chimpanzees and bonobos have been observed to hunt cooperatively and to share meat.

3. _____ *Homo habilis* learned how to use fire at the same time as it developed Oldowan tools.

4. _____ Hominines became bipedal at about the same time as their brain size radically increased.

5. _____ There is some dispute about the relationship between the Neanderthal and ourselves.

6. _____ According to Haviland, the chimpanzees and bonobos represent a accurate model for the behavior of our own ancient ancestors.

7. _____ Chimpanzees and bonobos are the most skilled of the apes in manipulating objects.

8. _____ According to the researchers involved in Project Chantek, an orangutan can tell lies.

9. _____ Chantek, the orangutan, although extremely intelligent, showed no evidence of the ability to take the perspective of others, nor was there evidence of intentionality, premeditation, or displacement in his behavior. Moreover, evidence was lacking for the symbolic use of language.

10. _____ Because the orangutans have retained more of the characteristics of the ancestral hominoid they have been labeled a "living fossil," and thus are a kind of time traveler.

11. _____ Cognitive studies with orangutans have shown that they are not as intelligent as the African apes.

12. _____ Orangutans are the escape artists of zoos because of their ability to manipulate bolts and wires to get out of their enclosures.

13. _____ There is evidence that orangutans, gorillas, and chimpanzees can develop language skills at the level of a five to six-year-old human child.

14. _____ Chantek understood that things had characteristics or attributes that could be described.

15. _____ Another component of the capacity to use symbols is displacement: the ability to refer to things or events not present. Chantek never could sign for things that were not present.

16. _____ No living primate represents a precise analogue for the behavior of our own ancient ancestors.

17. _____ Among chimps, all offspring are fathered by dominant males.

18. _____ In most primate species, females and their offspring constitute the core of the social system.

19. _____ Anatomical adaptation is import to primates because it is the only way they have of coping with the environment.

20. _____ Sexual activity among chimpanzees and bonobos occurs only during the period of each month when the female is fertile.

21. _____ Chimpanzees and bonobos are strictly vegetarians. They refrain from eating any meat.

22. _____ The most sophisticated example of teamwork in hunting occurs among the orangutan.

Answers to true/false practice questions

1. T	7. F	13. F	19. F
2. T	8. T	14. T	20. T
3. F	9. F	15. F	21. F
4. F	10. T	16. T	22. F
5. T	11. F	17. F	
6. F	12. T	18. T	

Practice Matching

1. _____ *Homo habilis*
2. _____ *Homo erectus*
3. _____ *Australopithecus*
4. _____ sivapithecines
5. _____ *Homo sapiens*

a. Learned to use fire.
b. First biped.
c. First stone tool maker.
d. Spread to Australia and the Americas.
e. A human-ape ancestor.

Answers to practice matching

1. c   2. a   3. b   4. e   5. d

Practice Essays

1. If you had to pick three to six key developments in the evolution of culture, what would they be? Write an essay identifying their importance to culture as we know among human beings.

2. What one question do you feel remains unanswered about the evolution of humans and human culture? That is, if you could make one key discovery, what would it be? Why would it be critical to our understanding of evolution?

3. From the study of both ancient and modern primates, anthropologists have worked out a list of anatomical characteristics common to them all. Identify those characteristics and explain how each facilitated the adaptation to an arboreal environment.

4. Compare and contrast the behavior of chimpanzees and bonobos, the closest genetic relatives to humans.

5. Describe chimpanzee patterns of behavior and discuss how they might have contributed to the emergence of human cultural behavior.

6. What was Project Chantek? Discuss its goals and findings.

7. Discuss the significance of meat eating and stone tool making for human evolution.

8. Discuss the importance of gathering in the evolution of human culture. Whose responsibility was gathering? What carrying devices were invented to gather foodstuff. These early carry devices evolved into some modern carrying devices. Identify and discuss the evolution of carrying devices that are in use today.

9. Important though anatomical adaptation has been to the primates, it has not been the only way primates have coped with their environment. Using examples, describe other ways primates have adapted to their environment?

10. Evidence indicates that at least one population of archaic *Homo sapiens* evolved into modern humans. Identify that population and describe what made them different from earlier forms of the genus *Homo*.

Chapter 4
Language and Communication

Synopsis

Chapter 4 introduces the field of anthropological linguistics, considering how existing languages are described and studied and what the history of language can tell us. It examines how language is related to culture and explores the evolution of the capacity for language. An extensive technical vocabulary relating to linguistics is presented.

What You Should Learn from This Chapter

1. Know how humans communicate with one another.

2. Know what linguistics is and the components of language.

3. Understand how humans use paralanguage to communicate.

4. Understand how humans use kinesics to communicate.

5. Know how ethnolinguistics aids in understanding culture.

6. Know the explanations offered about the origin of language.

Key Terms

bound morphemes

code switching

core vocabulary

dialects

displacement

ethnolinguistics

form classes

frame substitution

free morpheme

glottochronology

grammar

kinesics

language

language family

linguistic divergence

linguistic nationalism

linguistics

morphemes

paralanguage

phonemes

phonetic

phonology

signal

sociolinguistics

symbol

syntax

theory of linguistic relativity

vocal characterizers

vocal qualifiers

vocal segregates

vocalizations

voice qualities

Review Questions

1. Why is language so important to culture?

2. What is the anatomical "price we pay" for our vocal capabilities?

3. What does primatologist Allison Jolly mean by the "audience effect" she observes among the primates she studies?

4. Distinguish between a morpheme and a phoneme and give an example of each.

5. Distinguish between bound and free morphemes and give examples of each.

6. What is the function of frame substitution?

7. What is the purpose of a form class?

8. What method does descriptive linguistics use?

9. What is paralanguage? Provide examples.

10. What are the characteristic differences in body posture between men and women?

11. What is the "gesture-call" system?

12. What are the elements of voice quality?

13. Distinguish between vocal characterizers and vocal qualifiers.

14. How are gender markers employed?

15. What is code switching? Give an example you have observed.

16. What does glottochronology seek to explain?

17. Describe the importance of language for group identity.

18. What does ethnolinguistics seek to explain?

19. Provide an example that would support the theory of linguistic relativity.

20. What is meant by color-naming behavior?

21. How can linguists use metaphor as a key to understanding culture?

22. Why do linguists study kinship terms?

23. Haviland notes that wild speculation about the origins of language is no longer necessary. What advances have been made that make such speculation unnecessary?

24. What types of communication have primates been taught?

25. What are the communicative capabilities of monkeys and apes?

26. What is the difference between a signal and a symbol?

Fill-in-the-Blank

1. There are about _____ languages in the world.

2. A symbol has an arbitrary meaning determined by cultural convention, while a _____ has a natural or self-evident meaning.

3. Of all the potential sounds that can be made by the human vocal system, no more than _____ are used by any particular language.

4. The modern scientific study of language by Europeans began in the _____ with the collection of information about exotic languages by European explorers, invaders, and missionaries.

5. _____ is the systematic study of the production, transmission, and reception of speech sounds.

6. The smallest class of sound that makes a difference in meaning is called a _____.

7. The smallest significant unit of sound that carries a meaning is called a _____.

8. The entire formal structure of a language is called its _____.

9. The method used to define the rules and regularities of a language is called frame _____.

10. _____ refers to the extralinguistic noises that accompany language.

11. Voice _____ are the background characteristics of a speaker's voice that convey the state of the speaker.

12. Sounds such as "shh" and "uh-huh" that are similar to speech sounds but do not appear in sequences that can be called words are vocal _____.

13. _____ is usually referred to as "body language."

14. _____ linguistics studies relationships between earlier and later languages.

15. English belongs to the _____ language family.

16. Linguistic _____ refers to the attempt by nations to proclaim their independence and and distinctive identity by celebrating their own language.

17. The study of the relationship between language and social factors is called _____.

18. The process by which a person changes from one level of language to another is called _____.

Multiple-Choice Practice Questions

1. A system of communication based on symbols is called a _____.
   a. signal.
   b. form class.
   c. language.
   d. frame substitution.
   e. vocalization.

2. All languages are organized on the same basic plan in that _____.
   a. they are all based on signals.
   b. they take no more than fifty sounds and put them together in meaningful ways according to rules that can be determined by linguists.
   c. they take no more than three thousand sounds and organize them according to the rules of grammar.
   d. they all evolved from a common Egyptian language.
   e. they originated in Russia.

3. The modern scientific study of all aspects of language is _____.
   a. kinesics.
   b. phonology.
   c. linguistics.
   d. grammar.
   e. glottochronology.

4. The systematic study of the production, transmission, and reception of speech sounds is _____.
   a. linguistics.
   b. morphology.
   c. frame substitution.
   d. phonetics.
   e. syntax.

5. Paralanguage is to speech as _____ is to position of the body.
   a. kinesics
   b. ethnolinguistics
   c. form class
   d. phonetics
   e. displacement

6. Consider the English word "dog." Which of the following is a morpheme?
   a. "d"
   b. "dog"
   c. "o"
   d. "g"
   e. all of the above

7. The sounds *s* and *z* in "cats" and "dogs" are examples of _____.
   a. allophones.
   b. allomorphs.
   c. free morphemes.
   d. bound morphemes.
   e. signals.

8. The method called frame substitution enables the linguist to establish the rules or principles by which language users construct phrases and sentences, that is, the _____ of the language.
   a. morphology
   b. form classes
   c. core vocabulary
   d. sociolinguistics
   e. syntax

9. Two people say to you, "You sure look nice today." Although they are saying the same words, you can tell that one person is being complimentary and the other sarcastic by their _____.
   a. vocalizations.
   b. vocal characteristics.
   c. voice qualities.
   d. voice segregates.
   e. vocal qualifiers.

10. Kinesics is a method for notating and analyzing _____.
   a. screaming.
   b. kissing.
   c. any form of body 'language.'
   d. fighting.
   e. food.

11. Descriptive linguistics_____.
    a. attempts to explain the features of a particular language at one time in its history.
    b. looks at languages as separate systems without considering how they might be related to each other.
    c. attempts to construct a language's historical development.
    d. investigates relationships between earlier and later forms of the same language.
    e. *a* and *b* only

12. A language family is a group of languages that _____.
    a. all have the same core vocabulary.
    b. are subordinate to a dominant language.
    c. all have the same syntax.
    d. use the same number of sounds.
    e. are descended from a single ancestral language.

13. If the core vocabulary of two languages is compared by glottochronologists, it is thought possible to determine _____.
    a. if the two languages perceive reality in the same way.
    b. if the two languages use the same syntax.
    c. if they share the same allophones.
    d. if they have a similar technology.
    e. how long ago the languages separated from each other.

14. Which of the following statements about linguistic divergence is **incorrect**?
    a. One force for linguistic change is borrowing by one language from another.
    b. If languages were isolated from each other, there would be very little linguistic change.
    c. New vocabulary emerges in a language due to quest for novelty and the development of specialized vocabulary by groups.
    d. Changes in pronunciation may emerge as markers of class boundary (e.g., upper-class"U" versus "Non-U").
    e. Dying languages may be revived in the name of linguistic nationalism.

15. Which of the following is **not** an example of linguistic nationalism?
    a. You are a Spanish-speaking person in the United States and want your children to learn English, so that they can assimilate more completely into the society around them.
    b. A national committee in France declares that certain widely used terms will no longer be allowed to appear in public print because they are not French.
    c. You live in Scotland and are so alarmed by the rapid decline in the number of people speaking Gaelic that you start a school in which all subjects are taught in Gaelic.
    d. The southern part of India declares itself a separate country called Tamiland (the land of the people who speak Tamil) in defiance of India's declaration of Hindi as the national language; people say they will die in defense of their "mother tongue."
    e. A country previously colonized by the British passes a law requiring everyone to speak the native tongue; English is banned because of its association with colonial domination.

16. The influence of a person's class status on what pronunciation he/she uses; a speaker's choice of more complicated vocabulary and grammar when he/she is speaking to a professional audience; the influence of language on culture-all these are the concerns of _____.
    a. descriptive linguistics.
    b. historical linguistics.
    c. ethnolinguistics.
    d. linguistic nationalism.
    e. displacement.

17. Which of the following statements about the theory of linguistic relativity is **incorrect**?
    a. It was first formulated by Edward Sapir and Benjamin Whorf.
    b. It may be briefly explained with the sentence, "Language determines the reality that speakers of the language perceive."
    c. It may be briefly explained with the sentence, "Language reflects reality; it only mirrors what people perceive."
    d. It is expressed in this example: If in a factory a metal drum is labeled "empty" (when in fact it is filled with flammable fumes), people will perceive it as empty and may do things with it that may create a fire hazard (such as storing it near a furnace); but if it is labeled "full" of gaseous fumes, people will perceive it as a fire hazard and treat it more carefully.
    e. none of the above is incorrect

18. The term _____ is usually used to refer to varying forms of a language that reflect particular regions or social classes and that are similar enough to be mutually intelligible.
    a. dialect
    b. language subgroup
    c. language family
    d. linguistic nationalism
    e. linguistic relativity

19. On April 10, 1984, the _____ became the first community of Native Americans in the United States to affirm the right of its members to regain and maintain fluency in the ancestral language.
    a. Southern Paiute
    b. Northern Paiute
    c. Northern Ute
    d. Isleta Pueblo
    e. Apache

20. The very names for this dialect reflect the diversity of views. Which of the following are **not** terms used to refer to Ebonics.
    a. African American English (AAE)
    b. African American Vernacular (AAVE)
    c. Black English (BE)
    d. African American Dialect (AAD)
    e. they are all terms that refer to Ebonics.

21. Which of the following is **not** true of Black English?
    a. It has a short history.
    b. It has logical rules of grammar.
    c. Its discourse practices cannot be traced.
    d. It has an oral literature worthy of respect.
    e. *a* and *c*

22. A specialty within linguistic anthropology that has become almost a separate field of inquiry is _____.
    a. sociolinguistics.
    b. historical linguistics.
    c. ethnolinguistics.
    d. descriptive linguistics.
    e. kinesics.

23. The theory of linguistic relativity was once known as the _____.
    a. Edward-Benjamin hypothesis.
    b. Haviland hypothesis.
    c. theory of cultural relativity.
    d. theory of linguistic divergence.
    e. Sapir-Whorf hypothesis.

24. Although we are genetically programmed to speak, what we speak is determined by our _____.
    a. parents.
    b. teachers.
    c. linguists.
    d. culture.
    e. genetic make-up.

25. The first step in studying any language, once a number of utterances have been collected, is to isolate the _____.
    a. verbs.
    b. nouns.
    c. phonemes.
    d. adjectives.
    e. adverbs.

26. One of the strengths of modern descriptive linguistics is the _____ of its methods.
    a. subjectivity
    b. clarity
    c. objectivity
    d. simplicity
    e. consistency

27. In North America scratching one's scalp, biting one's lip, or knitting one's brows are ways of conveying doubt. They are also what linguists call _____.
    a. morphology.
    b. phonology.
    c. sociolinguistic.
    d. kinesics.
    e. sign language.

28. This approach concentrates on the way languages function now, as if they were separate systems, consistent within themselves, without any reference to historical reasons for their development.
    a. descriptive linguistics
    b. glottochronology
    c. diachronic linguistics
    d. historical linguistics
    e. phonology

29. _____ proposed that a language is not simply an encoding process for voicing our ideas and needs but, rather, is a shaping force, which, by providing habitual grooves of expression that predispose people to see the world in a certain way, guides their thinking and behavior.
    a. Benjamin Lee Whorf
    b. Noah Chomsky
    c. Paul Bohannan
    d. Emile Durkheim
    e. Robbins Burling

Answers to multiple-choice practice questions

1. c	9. c	17. c	25. c
2. b	10. c	18. a	26. c
3. c	11. e	19. c	27. d
4. d	12. e	20. d	28. a
5. a	13. e	21. e	29. a
6. b	14. b	22. c	
7. d	15. a	23. e	
8. e	16. c	24. d	

True/False Practice Questions

1. _____ Haviland traces linguistics back to the ancient grammarians in China more than three thousand years ago.

2. _____ Glottochronology assumes that the rate at which a language's core vocabulary changes is variable and thus cannot be used to give an exact date for when two languages diverged.

3. _____ Human culture as we know it could have easily existed without language.

4. _____ Though men and women in North American culture typically utilize slightly different vocabularies, the body language they use does not differ much.

5. _____ The emphasis on the French language by Quebecois separatists is an example of linguistic nationalism.

6. _____ "Ebonics" is a substandard or defective dialect of English.

7. _____ The Oakland Public Schools wanted to teach Black English in its schools.

8. _____ There was a sense of outrage among some that a stigmatized variety of English would be treated as a valid way of talking in the Oakland Public Schools.

9. _____ There is really very little difference between Black English (BE) and Standard English (SE).

10. _____ The Oakland school board wrongfully concluded that teachers needed to understand the differences between Standard English and Black English to properly teach children.

11. _____ Black English is not just some random form of "broken-down English" intrinsically inferior to Standard English but is a speech variety with its own long history.

12. _____ The problem with Black English is that its rules of grammar are illogical.

13. _____ Black English has discourse practices traceable to West African languages and a vibrant oral literature worthy of respect.

14. _____ In general, Black English has not added much to the vocabulary of American English.

15. _____ A major criticism of the Oakland school board's proposal to teach Ebonics is that teachers would be wasting time "teaching" African American Vernacular English when kids should be learning Standard English.

16. _____ According to linguistic anthropologist Ron Kephart, the most important work that anthropologists and linguists have to do is to raise public awareness and understanding of what linguistic, cultural and biological differences mean, and most importantly, what they don't mean.

17. _____ What the Oakland School Board proposed in regards to teaching Ebonics is no different from what is being done, with considerable success, in several other countries.

18. _____ No language uses more than about 100 sounds to communicate.

19. _____ Human language is always embedded within a gesture-call system of a type we share with monkeys and apes.

20. _____ Cross-cultural research has shown few similarities around the world for such basic facial expressions as smiling, laughing, crying, and variations of anger.

Answers to true/false practice questions

1. F	6. F	11. T	16. T
2. F	7. F	12. F	17. T
3. T	8. T	13. T	18. F
4. F	9. F	14. F	19. T
5. T	10. F	15. T	20. F

Practice Matching

Match the term to its definition.

1. _____bound morpheme

2. _____phonemes

3. _____form classes

4. _____kinesics

5. _____glottochronology

a. A method of dating divergence within language families.

b. The smallest classes of sound that make a difference in meaning.

c. A sound that occurs in a language only in combination with other sounds, as *s* in English to signify the plural.

d. Postures, facial expressions, and body motion.

e. The parts of speech that work the same in any sentence.

Answers to practice matching

1. c   2. b   3. e   4. d   5. a

Practice Essays

1. Would it be accurate to claim language as a distinguishing feature of *H. sapiens*? Why or why not? What evidence exists for the uniqueness or non-uniqueness of human language?

2. How is language linked to gender? Use examples from the text and add some of your own.

3. Discuss the "Great Ebonics Controversy." What are the arguments of the proponents of Ebonics? What are the arguments of those who oppose Ebonics?

4. What was the Northern Ute Language Renewal Project?

5. Of central importance to the development of human culture is language. How might language have started in the first place.

6. What is the theory of linguistic relativity? What do its detractors say about it?

7. Gender language reveals how women and men relate to each other. Exactly what does it reveal about how women and men relate?

Chapter 5
Growing Up Human

Synopsis

Chapter 5 focuses on how culture is transmitted from one generation to the next and explores the cultural contexts in which personalities are formed. It suggests a relativistic understanding of normality and abnormality and looks at recent changes in the field of psychological anthropology.

What You Should Learn from This Chapter

1. Understand the process and agents of enculturation.

2. Understand how the behavioral environment functions.

3. Understand how personality is shaped.

4. Understand the concepts of dependence and independence training in child rearing.

5. Know how group personality is determined.

6. Understand the purpose and criticism of national character studies.

7. Know how normality and abnormality are defined.

Key Terms and Names

core values

dependence training

enculturation

ethnic psychoses

group personality

independence training

Margaret Mead

mental illness

modal personality

national character

patterns of affect

personality

Ruth Fulton Benedict

self-awareness

Review Questions

1. Who are the agents of enculturation?

2. What are three aspects of self-awareness, according to Haviland?

3. Why might North American children's motor development lag behind that of children from non-Western societies?

4. What are three aspects of the behavioral environment?

5. What does the study of the Penobscot tell us about culture and personality?

6. Describe the situation of the Ju/'hoansi.

7. It was stated that what has seemed to be "normal" in the past, could become "abnormal" in the future. And conversely, it is also true that the abnormal may become the normal. What is meant by these statements?

8. Distinguish between dependence and independence training.

9. What did Margaret Mead's study of adolescent Samoans tell us?

10. Provide an example of modal personality.

11. Explain the basic statistics behind the concept of modal personality.

12. What purpose do the Rorschach and Thematic Appreception Tests serve?

13. What does Francis Hsu suggest are major personality traits of the Chinese?

14. What problems accompany the use of modal personality assessment?

15. What contribution did Ruth Benedict make to the field of culture-and-personality?

16. Why were national character studies undertaken?

17. What was Gorer's toilet-training hypothesis?

18. What are the major objections to national character studies?

19. Provide examples of core values.

20. What is the function of the *two-spirit* in Plains Indians society?

21. How are male and female role identities shaped by the structure of the human family, according to Nancy Chodorow?

22. How is abnormal behavior defined?

23. How are cures effected among the Melemchi of Nepal?

24. What is "windigo?"

Fill-in-the-Blank

1. The Enlightenment thinker John Locke presented the concept of _____ to express the idea that humans are born as "blank slates" and that everything depends on experience.

2. The term _____ refers to the process by which culture is transmitted from one generation to the next.

3. The Penobscot traditionally conceived of the self as divided into two parts, the body and the _____.

4. Margaret Mead studied three societies in _____ and found out that sex roles were highly variable.

5. Margaret Mead was a founder of the field called _____.

6. The Ju/'hoansi made a living by _____ in the Kalahari Desert.

7. A concept that attempted to retain the idea of a group personality and yet take into account the diversity of personalities within a group is the concept of _____.

8. The ink-blot test is properly called the _____ test.

9. The studies developed during World War II to explore the idea that modern nations could be characterized by personality types were called _____ studies.

10. The psychosis exhibited by northern Algonkian Indian groups who recognize the existence of cannibalistic monsters is called _____.

Exercise

Briefly identify the cultures listed below, and locate them on the world map.

1. Penobscot

2. Arapesh, Mundugamor, Tchambuli

3. Ju/'hoansi

4. Kwakiutl

5. Yanomami

6. Dobu

7. Melemchi

8. Algonkian Indians

Multiple-Choice Practice Questions

1. Enculturation is the process of transmitting _____.
   a. society from one generation to the next.
   b. social norms from one adult to another.
   c. culture from one child to another.
   d. culture from one generation to the next.
   e. personality from parent to child.

2. The agents of enculturation _____.
   a. are persons involved in transmitting culture to the next generation.
   b. are at first the members of the family into which the child is born.
   c. vary, depending on the structure of the family into which a child is born.
   d. include peer groups and schoolteachers.
   e. all of the above

3. Which of the following statements about self-awareness is **incorrect**?
   a. Self-awareness occurs earlier in children as a function of the amount of social stimulation they receive.
   b. At fifteen weeks of age, the home-reared infant in North America is in contact with its mother for about 20 percent of time.
   c. At fifteen weeks of age, infants in the Ju/'hoansi society of South Africa's Kalahari Desert are in close contact with their mothers about 70 percent of the time.
   d. American children develop self-awareness earlier than do Ju/'hoansi children.
   e. all of the above are correct

4. The _____ includes definitions and explanations of objects, spatial orientation, and temporal orientation, as well as culturally defined values, ideals, and standards that provide an individual with a normative orientation.
   a. vital self
   b. *tabula rasa*
   c. behavioral environment
   d. patterns of affect
   e. core values

5. In studying three societies in New Guinea, Margaret Mead found that the role played by men and women were determined primarily by _____.
   a. genes.
   b. biology.
   c. culture.
   d. incest.
   e. the food they ate.

6. Margaret Mead's groundbreaking work in culture and personality published in 1928 was a deliberate test of a Western psychological hypothesis. What was this hypothesis?
   a. Lowering the drinking age will promote promiscuity.
   b. Child-rearing practices have no effect on adult personality.
   c. The stress and conflict experienced by American adolescents is a universal phenomenon based on maturing hormones.
   d. By changing child-rearing practices, we can change the structure of society.
   e. By lowering the driving age, we can promote less stress among adolescents.

7. A study of child rearing among the Ju/'hoansi of Africa indicates that _____.
   a. boys and girls are raised in a very similar manner and are both mild-mannered and self-reliant.
   b. because girls are out gathering most of the time, they are expected to be more aggressive and self-reliant than boys are.
   c. mothers spend the least amount of time with their children, and thus the children identify strongly with their fathers.
   d. boys do more work than girls.
   e. boys have less responsibility than girls and get to play more of the time.

8. Independence training, according to Child and Whitings, is more likely in _____.
   a. small nuclear families.
   b. large extended families.
   c. small-scale horticultural societies where a man has many wives.
   d. a pastoralist family where a woman has many husbands and the extended family has to be always on the move.
   e. New York City neighborhoods where large families stay nearby and support each other.

9. Dependence training is more likely in _____.
   a. nuclear families.
   b. societies whose subsistence is based on pastoralism.
   c. a food-foraging society.
   d. extended families in societies whose economy is based on subsistence farming.
   e. industrial societies.

10. The personality typical of a society, as indicated by the central tendency of a defined frequence distribution, is called _____.
    a. core values.
    b. nuclear personality.
    c. patterns of affect.
    d. culture and personality.
    e. modal personality.

11. Which of the following statements about modal personality is correct?
    a. Although a modal personality may be found for a particular society, a range of personalities may exist in that society.
    b. Although the modal personality may be considered "normal" for that society, it may be shared by less than half of the population.
    c. Those who study modal personality accept the fact that there may be abnormal individuals in that society.
    d. Data on modal personality are usually gathered by the use of psychological tests such as the Rorschach and TAT.
    e. all of the above are correct

12. Studies of _____ were developed during World War II to explore the idea that basic personality traits were shared by most of the people in modern nations.
    a. modal personality
    b. national character
    c. stereotype
    d. group personality
    e. independence training

13. The term "core values" refers to _____.
    a. those aspects of culture that pertain to the way a culture makes its living.
    b. rules that guide family and home life.
    c. those values emphasized by a particular culture.
    d. common shares in Golden Delicious Corp.
    e. the beliefs stressed by a particular political party.

14. Among the Plains Indians, a man who wore women's clothes, performed women's work, and married another man _____.
    a. was considered normal.
    b. was sought out as a curer, artist, and matchmaker.
    c. was assumed to have great spiritual power.
    d. might have been homosexual.
    e. all of the above

15. An ethnic psychosis refers to a _____.
    a. psychotic episode experienced by a person from an exotic culture.
    b. progressive disease that strikes anthropologists when they spend more than twelve months in the field.
    c. psychosis characterized by symptoms peculiar to a particular group.
    d. universal form of mental illness.
    e. biologically based disease that resembles schizophrenia.

16. Traditional culture and personality studies _____.
    a. were important in undermining ethnocentrism.
    b. are criticized today for being impressionistic and difficult to replicate.
    c. diversified the study of psychological processes in a cultural context.
    d. promoted a relativistic point of view.
    e. all of the above

17. According to your textbook, among the Yanomami _____.
    a. all men are fierce and warlike.
    b. all men are quiet and retiring.
    c. there is a range of personalities.
    d. a quiet, retiring Yanomamo would not survive.
    e. a fierce, warlike Yanomamo would not survive.

18. In _____ infants generally do not sleep with their parents, most often being put in rooms of their own. This is seen as an important step in making them into individuals, "owners" of themselves and their capacities, rather than part of some social whole.
    a. the Ituri rain forest
    b. China
    c. the United States
    d. Mexico
    e. the Kalahari Desert

19. As _____ pioneering studies suggested, whatever biological differences may exist between men and women, they are extremely malleable.
    a. Ruth Benedict's
    b. Karen Sacks's
    c. Deborah Tannen's
    d. Margaret Mead's
    e. Laura Nader's

20. One of the "founding mothers" of anthropology is _____.
    a. Nancy Scheper-Hughes
    b. Catherine Bateson
    c. Mary Douglas
    d. Margaret Mead
    e. Emily Schultz

21. Today in Native American societies the preferred term to describe an individual who falls between the categories of "man" and "woman" is known as _____.
    a. berdache.
    b. gay.
    c. passive homosexual.
    d. two-spirit.
    e. effeminate.

22. We should not be surprised to find that explanations of the universe are never entirely objective in nature, but are _____.
    a. culturally constructed.
    b. figments of one's imagination.
    c. scientifically constructed.
    d. evolved historically.
    e. simply absurd.

23. Usually regarded as dreaded liabilities, anthropologist _____ suggests that, in North America, aspects of manic-depression and Attention Deficit Hyperactivity Disorder (ADHD), are coming to be seen as assets in the quest for success.
    a. Jennifer Thompson
    b. Vicki Cassman
    c. Emily Martin
    d. Martha Knack
    e. William Jankowiak

24. All societies must somehow ensure that their culture is adequately transmitted from one generation to the next. This transmission process is known as _____.
    a. acculturation.
    b. assimilation.
    c. enculturation.
    d. absorption.
    e. integration.

25. When first encountered by Europeans, the _____ conceived of each individual as being made of two parts-the body and a personal spirit.
    a. Apache
    b. Onondaga
    c. Penobscot
    d. Menominee
    e. Iroquois

26. The _____ personality is the personality typical of a society as indicated by the central tendency of a defined frequency distribution.
    a. normal
    b. average
    c. standard
    d. mean
    e. modal

27. Data on modal personality are best gathered with psychological tests administered to a sample of the population in question. Those most often used would include which of the following?
    a. SAT
    b. Rorschach, or inkblot test
    c. DAP (Draw a Person Test)
    d. TAT (thematic Apperception Test)
    e. only *b* and *d*

28. Among the _____, a widely held belief is that spirits are active in the world and that they influence human behavior.
    a. Germans
    b. French
    c. Argentinians
    d. Puerto Ricans
    e. Spanish

29. _____ is a fear reaction often occurring in middle-aged Malay women of low intelligence who are subservient and self-effacing.
    a. Koro
    b. Saka
    c. Windigo
    d. Pibloktoq
    e. Latah

Answers to multiple-choice practice questions

1. d	9. d	17. c	25. c
2. e	10. e	18. c	26. e
3. d	11. e	19. d	27. e
4. c	12. b	20. d	28. d
5. c	13. c	21. d	29. e
6. c	14. e	22. a	
7. a	15. c	23. c	
8. a	16. e	24. c	

True/False Practice Questions

1. _____ What is considered "normal" in a society is defined by culture.

2. _____ Anthropologists believe that all mental illness is learned rather than biologically based.

3. _____ Both hunting and gathering societies and industrial societies promote independence training in their mobile nuclear families.

4. _____ Margaret Mead believed that male and female roles were by and large defined by the biological attributes of the sexes.

5. _____ National character studies developed during World War II to explore the idea that basic personality traits were shared by most of the people in modern nations.

6. _____ The primary contribution of Whiting and Child to the field of psychological anthropology was their in-depth study of the Ju/'hoansi.

7. _____ The Yanomami of Brazil are known for their "fierceness," yet there is a range of personality types even there.

8. _____ The Native American view sees intersexed individuals in a very positive and affirming light.

9. _____ The Euro-American view of intersexed individuals is similar to the Native American view.

10. _____ The extent to which Native Americans see spirituality is reflected in their belief that all things have spirit.

11. _____ From the Native American perspective the spirit of a human is superior to the spirit of any other thing.

12. _____ To Native Americans the function of religion is not to try to condemn or to change what exists, but to accept the realities of the world and to appreciate their contributions.

13. _____ Native American believe everything that exists has a purpose.

14. _____ An intersexed child is derided and viewed as a "freak of nature" in traditional Native American culture.

15. _____ What was abnormal in the past may become normal.

16. _____ Today, for a man to assume a feminine identity is not regarded as abnormal by European-Americans; in fact, such individuals are regarded as special in that they bridge the gap between the purely feminine and purely masculine.

17. _____ In food-foraging societies child-rearing practices combine elements of both dependence and independence training.

18. _____ As hard as they have tried, anthropologists have never found a quiet and retiring Yanomami man.

19. _____ What defines normal behavior in any culture is determined by the culture itself, and what may be acceptable, or even admirable, in one may not be in another.

Answers to true/false practice questions

1. T	6. F	11. F	16. F
2. F	7. T	12. T	17. T
3. T	8. T	13. T	18. F
4. F	9. F	14. F	19. T
5. T	10. T	15. T	

Practice Essays

1. It was stated that what has seemed to be "normal" in the past, could become "abnormal" in the future. And conversely, it is also true that the abnormal may become the normal. What is meant by these statements? Provide examples.

2. What was the impact of Freudian psychoanalysis on the development of psychological anthropology? How have culture-and-personality specialists responded to the Freudian paradigm?

3. What is the traditional Penobscot concept of self? What did it have to do with their behavioral environment?

4. The author of the original study The Blessed Curse mentioned, "from a very early age I was presented with two different and conflicting views of myself." What did the author mean by this? Explain.

5. Explain why the Native American and Euro-American views on intersexuality are so diametrically opposed.

6. Discuss the importance of child-rearing practices for the development of gender related personality characteristics. Provide examples.

7. Explain why child rearing practices in the United States creates problems of gender identity for both sexes, although a different sort for each sex.

8. How does a culture itself induce certain kinds of psychological conflicts that have important consequences for the entire society?

9. The original study is entitled "The Blessed Curse: A Foot in Both Worlds." What is the explanation for this rather unusual title?

10. Using examples, explain the importance of a child-rearing practices in the development of gender-related personality characteristics.

11. How does a society's economy help structure the way a child is brought up and how does this, influence the development of the adult personality?

Chapter 6
Patterns of Subsistence

Synopsis

In Chapter 6 the text examines the impact that various modes of subsistence have on cultures. Food foraging is described in detail, and the variations in food production systems are discussed.

What You Should Learn from This Chapter

1. Understand the role of adaptation in cultural survival:
   - unit of adaptation
   - evolutionary adaptation
   - culture areas
   - culture core

2. Understand the food-foraging way of life:
   - subsistence and sex roles
   - food sharing
   - cultural adaptations and material technology
   - egalitarian society

3. Understand food-producing society:
   - horticulturalist
   - pastoralist
   - intensive agriculture and preindustrial cities

Key Terms and Names

adaptation

carrying capacity

convergent evolution

cultural ecology

culture area

culture core

culture type

density of social relations

ecosystem

ethnoscientists

horticulture

Julian Steward

parallel evolution

pastoralist

preindustrial cities

swidden

Review Questions

1. What purpose does adaptation serve?

2. Describe the relationship the Tsembaga have with the environment.

3. Explain what is meant by a unit of adaptation.

4. What are human ecologists concerned with?

5. Describe Comanche adaptation to the plains environment.

6. Distinguish between convergent and parallel evolution.

7. Provide an example of how a culture can be stable while not necessarily static.

8. Discuss the findings of Ann Kendall's research?

9. Why did native groups on the plains not farm?

10. What is the role of the ethnoscientist?

11. About how many people currently live by food foraging?

12. What previously held misconceptions of food foragers have been refuted?

13. What are the main social characteristics of food foragers?

14. What are the size-limiting factors in a foraging group?

15. What purpose does population redistribution serve for the Ju/'hoansi?

16. What impact does biological sex have on the division of labor?

17. How is the behavior of food-foraging groups reflected in their material culture?

18. Why are food foragers generally egalitarian?

19. Can we make any generalizations about the status of women in foraging societies?

20. How is territory conceptualized in foraging societies?

21. Define the concerns of Julian Steward's study of cultural ecology.

22. Distinguish between horticulturalists and intensive agriculturalists.

23. What are the basic features of pastoralist society?

24. Define "adaptation" and "ecosystem" and illustrate the relevance of these concepts with the example of pig sacrifices among the Tsembaga.

25. Why has slash-and-burn (swidden) come to be viewed negatively by many people today?

26. Describe the subsistence practices of the Mekranoti.

27. What did anthropologist Ann Kendall learn from the past mistakes of indigenous peoples of the Patacacha Valley in the Andes Mountains of southern Peru?

Fill-in-the-Blank

1. _____ is the process by which organisms modify and adjust to their environment and thereby survive more effectively.

2. The main animal raised by the Gururumba is _____.

3. When the Comanche migrated to the Great Plains, they found a new food source, the _____.

4. When several societies with different cultural backgrounds move into a new environment and develop similar adaptations, they represent the cultural equivalent of _____ evolution.

5. When several societies with very similar cultural backgrounds develop along similar lines, they represent the process of _____ evolution.

6. A geographic region in which a number of different societies follow a similar pattern of life is called a culture _____.

7. The various societies of the Great Plains had common religious rituals, such as _____.

8. The subfield within anthropology that studies the interaction of specific cultures with their environments is called _____.

9. The anthropologist who pioneered this subfield was _____.

10. _____ try to understand folk ideologies and how they help a group survive.

11. Humans lived using food foraging until about _____ years ago, when domestication of animals and plants began.

12. The Ju/'hoansi of the Kalahari Desert have been called "the original _____ society" because they work so few hours a week.

13. The number of people who can be supported by a certain technology is the _____ of the environment.

14. About _____ percent of the diet of most food foragers is gathered by women.

15. Increased food sharing appears to be related to a shift in food habits involving increased eating of _____ around two and a half million years ago.

16. Another name for slash-and-burn is _____ farming.

17. The Bakhtiari of the Zagros Mountains are _____ who migrate seasonally from one location to another.

18. City life is based on a subsistence pattern of _____.

19. The main city of the Aztecs was _____.

20. The anthropologist who conducted her research in the Andes Mountains of southern Peru was _____.

Exercises

I. Complete the chart below, filling in examples of each type of subsistence and noting its general characteristics. You can use this to study from later.

PATTERNS OF SUBSISTENCE

Type	Example	Characteristics
Foraging		
Pastoralism		
Horticlture		
Intensive Agriculture		

II. Briefly identify the cultures listed below, and locate them on the world map.

1. Tsembaga

2. Comanche

3. Shoshone and Paiute

4. Hadza

5. Mekranoti

6. Gurumba

7. Bakhtiari

8. Innu

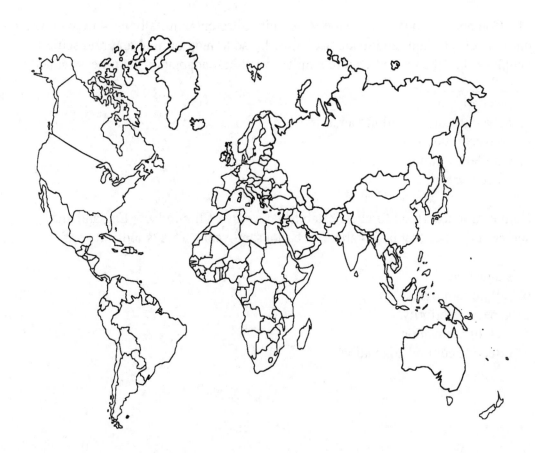

Multiple-Choice Practice Questions

1. Adaptation refers to the _____.
   a. process by which organisms modify and adjust to their environment and thereby survive more effectively.
   b. ability of one population to destroy another.
   c. borrowing of cultural material from another society.
   d. process by which living systems change from birth to death.
   e. effect of child-rearing practices on basic personality structure.

2. Before the arrival of horses and guns, the Comanche were food foragers in southern Idaho. Their skill as hunters was put to good use as they used these new tools to hunt buffalo on the Great Plains. The term used to refer to existing customs that by chance have potential for a new cultural adaptation is _____.
   a. convergent evolution.
   b. divergent evolutions.
   c. ecosystem.
   d. parallel evolution.
   e. preadaptations.

3. The Comanche and the Cheyenne were quite different culturally until they moved out onto the Great Plains and made use of the horse to hunt buffalo and raid settled peoples. They then became more similar in cultural adaptations, a process called
   _____.
   a. preadaptation.
   b. development of a culture area.
   c. convergent evolution.
   d. parallel evolution.
   e. an ecosystem.

4. Native American food foragers established a way of life in New England and southern Quebec that lasted about five thousand years. This is indicative of
   _____.
   a. stagnation.
   b. failure to progress.
   c. genetic inferiority.
   d. lack of innovation.
   e. effective cultural adaptation.

5. A culture type is defined by _____.
   a. the geographic area in which a people live.
   b. the kind of technology that a group has to exploit a particular environment.
   c. contacts with other cultures.
   d. sharing the same values.
   e. sharing the same language.

6. A taboo against eating certain foods, the belief that only a chief has strong enough magic to plant apple trees and dispense them to his fellow villagers, and the number of hours a people work each day are examples of what could be considered part of a society's _____.
   a. structural base.
   b. foundation.
   c. infrastructure.
   d. culture core.
   e. none of the above.

7. Which of the following research topics might be of interest to an ethnoscientist?
   a. How the allele responsible for sickle-cell anemia increases or decreases in certain cultural environments, such a horticultural vs. hunting-gathering.
   b. Similarities and differences in the farming patterns of Southwest Asia and Mesoamerica.
   c. The ways in which a group classifies and explains the world; for example, the Tsembaga avoid low-lying, marshy areas filled with mosquitoes that carry malaria because they believe that such areas are inhabited by red spirits who punish trespassers.
   d. Reconstruction and comparison of archaeological sites in similar geographic regions.
   e. all of the above

8. Some anthropologists refer to food foragers as "the original affluent society" because _____.
   a. they manage to accumulate a lot of wealth.
   b. they occupy the most attractive environments with abundant food supply.
   c. they live in marginal areas and are very poor.
   d. they earn a good wage for all hours of work they put in each week.
   e. they work only twelve to nineteen hours a week for a comfortable, healthy life.

9. The groups referred to as food foragers must live where there are naturally available food sources; thus they _____.
   a. remain in permanent settlements.
   b. move about once every ten years.
   c. move frequently.
   d. adopt farming whenever they can.
   e. prefer to live in cities.

10. The number and intensity of interactions among the members of a residential unit is called _____.
    a. density of social relations.
    b. social interactionism.
    c. cultural ecology.
    d. carrying capacity.
    e. convergent evolution.

11. Which of the following is **not** one of the three elements of human social organization that developed with hunting?
    a. sexual division of labor
    b. aggressive behavior
    c. food sharing
    d. the camp site
    e. all of the above

12. In a food-foraging society, how do people store food for the future?
    a. They keep a surplus in stone cairns.
    b. They keep extra plants in large, circular yam houses.
    c. They hide meat in each individual family residence.
    d. They rely on the generosity of others to share food.
    e. They keep dried food in a common storage shed.

13. To say that food-foraging societies are egalitarian means that _____.
    a. there are no status differences.
    b. the only status differences are age and sex.
    c. everyone is equal except women.
    d. men are usually subordinate to women.
    e. children are the center of community life.

14. Someone who uses irrigation, fertilizers, and the plow to produce food on large plots of land is known as a/an _____.
    a. horticulturalists.
    b. intensive agriculturalist.
    c. pastoralists.
    d. hunter-gatherer.
    e. industrialist.

15. _____ are food producers who specialize in animal husbandry and who consider their way of life to be ideal and central to defining their identities.
    a. Food foragers
    b. Horticulturalists
    c. Intensive agriculturalists
    d. Pastoralists
    e. Industrialists

16. Aztec society in the sixteenth century _____.
    a. was a stratified society based on achievement and education.
    b. was an urbanized society in which kinship played no role in determining status.
    c. was an industrial city-state.
    d. was invincible to Cortes' attack.
    e. none of the above

17. Which of the following statements about preindustrial cities is **incorrect**?
    a. Preindustrial cities have existed in some parts of the world for thousands of years.
    b. Preindustrial cities represent a stage of development in the progression of human culture toward industrial cities.
    c. Tenochtitlan, the capital of the Aztec empire, is a good example of a preindustrial city.
    d. Preindustrial cities have a diversified economy.
    e. Preindustrial cities are highly stratified.

18. This North American developed an approach that he called cultural ecology, that is, the interaction between specific cultures with their environments.
    a. Ann Kendall
    b. Leslie White
    c. Fred Plog
    d. Julian Steward
    e. Barbara Myerhoff

19. After three years of tending their gardens the Mekranoti are left with only
    _____.
    a. manioc.
    b. sweet potatoes.
    c. pineapple.
    d. tobacco.
    e. bananas.

20. A society's cultural beliefs, no matter how irrelevant they may seem to outsiders, are
    anything but irrelevant if one is to understand another society's _____
    practices.
    a. marketing
    b. voting
    c. business
    d. trading
    e. subsistence

21. How food-foraging peoples regulate population size relates to which of the following
    things?
    a. How much body fat they accumulate
    b. The accumulation of material goods
    c. Abortion practices
    d. How they care for their children
    e. *a* and *d*

22. Haviland points out in his textbook *Cultural Anthropology*, that _____ is
    an effective way of living-far more so than ranching.
    a. food-foraging
    b. pastoralism
    c. slash and burn agriculture
    d. hunting and gathering
    e. farming

23. The _____ process establishes a moving balance between the needs of a
    population and the potential of its environment.
    a. adaptation
    b. accommodation
    c. integration
    d. evolution
    e. adjustment

24. The kind of development where similar cultural adaptations to similar environmental conditions by peoples whose ancestral cultures were quite different is called

    _____.
    a. parallel evolution.
    b. complementary evolution.
    c. concurrent evolution.
    d. affinal evolution.
    e. convergent evolution.

25. _____ is the study of the interaction of specific human cultures with their environments.
    a. Ecological interaction
    b. Symbolic interaction
    c. Scientific ecology
    d. Social ecology
    e. Cultural ecology

26. The number of people the available resources can support at a given technological level is known as the _____.
    a. density of social relations.
    b. equilibrium point.
    c. carrying capacity.
    d. point of diminishing capacity.
    e. balanced position.

27. Food foragers like the _____ have a division of labor in which women gather and prepare "bush" food, but hunting is usually done by men.
    a. Gros Ventre
    b. Crow
    c. Ju/'hoansi
    d. Mandingo
    e. Tutsi

28. Although we tend to think of people as either food foragers or food producers, there are numerous examples of people like the _____, who rely on a mix of wild and domesticated resources.
    a. Ju/'hoansi
    b. Comanche
    c. Abenaki
    d. Pequot
    e. Papago

29. Aztec agricultural success provided for which of the following?
    a. a highly mobile population
    b. an increasingly large population
    c. the diversification of labor
    d. a more egalitarian society
    e. *b* and *c*

30. Intensive agriculture, a more complex activity than swidden farming, requires which of the following?
    a. irrigation
    b. fertilizers
    c. draft animals
    d. a high level of mobility
    e. all but *d*

Answers to multiple-choice practice questions

1. a	9. c	17. b	25. e
2. e	10. a	18. d	26. c
3. c	11. b	19. e	27. c
4. e	12. d	20. e	28. c
5. b	13. b	21. e	29. e
6. d	14. b	22. b	30. e
7. c	15. d	23. a	
8. e	16. e	24. e	

True/False Practice Questions

1. _____ According to the Original Study, the Mekranoti had to work hard to get enough produce from their gardens.

2. _____ The Mbuti live in the Ituri rain forest in the Republic of the Congo.

3. _____ The Bakhtiari are pastoralist nomads who drive their herds throughout the Iran-Iraq border area.

4. _____ Many Bakhtiari are well-educated, having attended university at home or aboard.

5. _____ The spread of malaria was historically linked to the development of slash-and-burn horticulture.

6. _____ In the world today about 3 million people live by food foraging.

7. _____ People started shifting to food-producing ways of life about ten thousand years ago.

8. _____ The average work week of the Ju/'hoansi is about fifty hours.

9. _____ An anthropologist would probably find it difficult to define what "progress" is.

10. _____ The Mekranoti style of slash-and-burn farming did not grow well because animals and insects were constantly invading their gardens.

11. _____ Due to their reliance of slash-and-burn farming the Mekranoti need to work very hard to survive.

12. _____ The Mekranoti constantly weed their gardens to keep the forest from invading.

13. _____ Slash-and-burn agriculture, especially in the humid tropics, may be one of the best gardening techniques possible.

14. _____ Anthropologists were the last to note the possibly disastrous consequences of U.S.-style agriculture in the tropics.

15. _____ According agriculturalists, open-field agriculture is less of a problem than slash-and-burn agriculture.

16. _____ The high fertility of Mekranoti garden plots comes from the soil, not from the trees that are burned there.

17. _____ Because of foraging animals and destructive insects, the Mekranoti could not depend on harvesting whatever they planted.

18. _____ The Mekranoti, it was found, don't have to work very hard to survive.

19. _____ Among food-foraging peoples teenage pregnancies are rampant.

20. _____ Food foraging would certainly not be found in a rich industrial nation such as the United States.

21. _____ Among food foragers today, the work of women is no less arduous than that of men.

22. _____ There are no sources of status differences among food foragers.

23. _____ Today we know that, especially in the humid tropics, slash-and-burn agriculture may be one of the best gardening techniques possible.

24. _____ It can be safely said that "preindustrial" cities are very uncommon in today's world.

Answer to true/false practice questions

1. F	7. T	13. T	19. F
2. T	8. F	14. F	20. F
3. T	9. T	15. F	21. T
4. T	10. F	16. F	22. F
5. T	11. F	17. F	23. T
6. F	12. F	18. T	24. F

Practice Matching

1. _____ Tsembaga   a. They live in Labrador.
2. _____ Bakhtiari   b. West Asian pastoralists.
3. _____ Comanche   c. Horse people of the Great Plains.
4. _____ Mbuti   d. Pig sacrificers of New Guinea.
5. _____ Innu   e. Food foragers of the Ituri rain forest.

Answers to practice matching

1. d   2. b   3. c   4. e   5. a

Practice Essays

1. How does Ju/'hoansi social organization relate to the subsistence pattern of hunting and collecting? How is Ju/'hoansi society likely to change as the foraging way of life erodes?

2. Think about your neighborhood. Could it be described as a kind of cultural area, i.e., a geographic region in which a number of different societies follow similar patterns of life? What criteria would be important for defining it that way?

3. The Mekranoti Kayapo employ what has come to be known as slash-and-burn agriculture. Describe the benefits of this style of farming in the tropics. What would be the consequences of a U.S.-style of agriculture in the tropics?

4. As mentioned in your textbook, just as we have much to learn from the successes of indigenous peoples, so can we learn from their mistakes, and the ways they cope with their mistakes. Anthropologist Ann Kendall is doing just this in southern Peru. What did her research discover and what is she doing to rectify the results of the past mistakes of indigenous peoples in the Patacacha Valley in the Andes Mountains?

5. Explain how the anthropologist was able to calculate the productivity of Mekranoti gardens.

6. It is said that "environments do not determine culture but do set certain potentials and limitations." Provide examples to support this statement.

7. What impact has intensive agriculture had on human society?

Chapter 7
Economic Systems

Synopsis

Chapter 7 discusses the attempt to apply economic theory to non-Western cultures and summarizes the concepts anthropologists have developed to compare the organization of productive resources across cultures. Three major ways of distributing goods and services are described. The relevance of anthropological understanding to international business is also considered.

What You Should Learn from This Chapter

1. Understand how anthropologists use theory to study economic systems.

2. Know the patterns of labor in nonindustrial societies:
   - sexual division of labor
   - division of labor by age
   - cooperation
   - craft specialization
   - control of land
   - technology

3. Understand the methods of distribution and exchange in nonindustrial societies:
   - reciprocity
   - redistribution
   - market exchange

Key Terms and Names

balanced reciprocity

Big Man

conspicuous consumption

generalized reciprocity

informal economy

Kula ring

leveling mechanism

market exchange

money

negative reciprocity

reciprocity

redistribution

silent trade

technology

Review Questions

1. Why might it be misleading to apply contemporary economic theories to preindustrial non-Western societies?

2. Explain the importance of yam production among the Trobrianders.

3. Provide examples that refute the notion of a biological division of labor.

4. Compare and contrast the three general patterns of the sexual division of labor.

5. What are the benefits of the division of labor?

6. How is land controlled in most preindustrial societies?

7. Differentiate between the use of tools in foraging, horticultural, and agricultural communities.

8. Distinguish between industrial and nonindustrial societies with regard to craft specialization.

9. How do societies cooperate in the acquisition of food?

10. Provide some examples of leveling mechanisms.

11. Distinguish between market exchange and marketplace.

12. What are three systems of exchange?

13. What purpose does reciprocity serve?

14. Differentiate between general, balanced, and negative reciprocity.

15. How is trade between groups generally conducted?

16. As discussed in your textbook, describe the relationships between the Kota, Toda, Badaga, and Kurumba of India.

17. What functions does the Kula ring serve?

18. Compare "money" among the Aztec and the Tiv.

19. Why is redistribution generally undertaken?

20. Describe the "informal economy" of North America.

21. How is conspicuous consumption used?

22. Discuss the relevance of anthropology to international business.

23. What are the drawbacks of ethnocentric interpretations of other societies' economic systems?

24. Discuss the role that culture plays in defining the "wants and needs" of a people.

Fill-in-the-Blank

1. All societies have rules pertaining to three productive resources: _____, _____, and _____.

2. Division of labor by sex varies from very flexible to very rigid. Among foragers like the _____, either sex may do the work of the other without loss of face.

3. Rigid division of labor by sex typically occurs with two patterns of subsistence: _____ and _____.

4. In most societies the basic unit in which cooperation takes place is the
   _____.

5. Among horticulturalists, tools that are typically used are the _____.

6. A _____ works to spread wealth around so that no one accumulates
   substantially more wealth than anyone else.

7. The economist _____ developed the threefold classification system of
   reciprocity, redistribution, and market exchange.

8. Types of reciprocity are _____, _____, and
   _____.

9. The taxation systems of Canada and the United States are examples of
   _____.

10. In some societies the surplus is used as a display for purposes of prestige. Thorsten
    Veblen called this _____.

11. Among the Enga of Papua New Guinea, the group that pools its wealth is the
    _____.

12. The Kota, Toda, Badaga, and Kurumba are interrelated societies in
    _____.

Exercises

I. When Bronislaw Malinowski studied the Kula ring of the Trobriand Islanders in his
    classic *Argonauts of the Western Pacific*, he also described other methods of
    distributing goods in that society as well. Consider each of the following examples of
    Trobriand exchanges given by Malinowski, and identify whether they can be
    characterized as forms of reciprocity, redistribution, or market exchange. Then note
    the elements of each of these forms of exchange in modern North American society
    as well.

    A. *Wasi:* permanent partnerships inland yam-producers inherit with fishermen.
        When a fisherman brings in a good catch, he takes some fish to his inland
        partner and gives them as a gift; when the farmer brings in his yam harvest, he
        takes some to the fisherman as a gift. Neither has any choice about changing
        partners, neither can bargain for more products, and there is no stated
        expectation of a return.

B. *Urigubu:* the yam gift that a man gives to his sister's husband every year; it is part of a person's kinship obligations.

C. *Kula:* the exchange between contractual partners of ceremonial/prestige/treasure items.

D. *Pokala:* tribute to a higher-status person, usually a chief.

E. *Sagali:* giveaway feast by a high-status person, usually a chief.

F. *Gim walli:* the moneyless exchange of mundane goods (barter) that occurs after the Kula gift-giving; this exchange occurs between anyone (no contractual partners), and the value seems to be established according to supply and demand and done with a desire to gain the greatest profit.

II. Briefly identify the following cultures, and indicate their locations on the map.

1. Enga

2. Inca

3. Afar

4. Tiv

5. Kota, Toda, Bagada, Kurumba

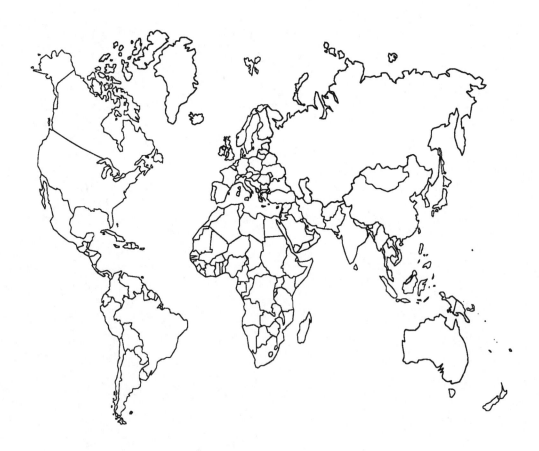

Multiple-Choice Practice Questions

1. When a man works hard in his horticultural garden in the Trobriand Islands to produce yams, he does this to satisfy which of the following demands?
   a. to have food for his household to eat
   b. to gain prestige by giving yams away to his sisters' husbands
   c. to prove to his wife that he can work as hard as she can
   d. to give the yams to his wife so that she can trade them for goods that they don't produce themselves
   e. to trade for fish

2. The productive resources used by all societies to produce goods and services include _____.
   a. raw materials.
   b. labor.
   c. technology.
   d. bureaucrats.
   e. all but *d*

3. American society's traditional sexual division of labor falls into which pattern?
   a. flexible
   b. rigid segregation
   c. segregation with equality
   d. integrated
   e. cooperative

4. Among the Ju/'hoansi _____.
   a. children are expected to contribute to subsistence from the time they are seven or eight.
   b. elderly people past the age of sixty are expected to contribute hunted or gathered food to the group.
   c. elderly people are a valuable source of knowledge and wisdom about hunting and gathering.
   d. elderly people are taken care of grudgingly because after the age of sixty they contribute nothing to the group.
   e. children are expected to set up their own separate households by the time they are twelve.

5. In many nonindustrial societies,
   a. people prefer to have fun rather than to work.
   b. cooperative work is usually done with a festive, sociable air.
   c. cooperative work is always done in the household.
   d. cooperative work groups are organized primarily for profit.
   e. solitary work is preferred to cooperative work.

6. Among food foragers such as the Ju/'hoansi,
   a. land is defined as a territory with usable resources and flexible boundaries that belongs to a band that has occupied it for a long time.
   b. land is thought of as belonging to those who have bought it.
   c. land is considered private property, and access to the land can be denied.
   d. land has clear-cut boundaries marked by survey posts.
   e. land is controlled by a corporation of strangers.

7. In nonindustrial societies, when a tool is complex and difficult to make it is usually considered to be owned by _____.
   a. the whole village in which it is used.
   b. a single individual.
   c. the state.
   d. all those who touch it.
   e. all relatives.

8. Leveling mechanisms _____.
   a. are more common in hunter-gatherer societies than in agricultural communities.
   b. result in one family becoming wealthier than others.
   c. are found in communities where property must not be allowed to threaten an egalitarian social order.
   d. are more common in industrial societies than in agricultural societies.
   e. no longer exist.

9. The mode of distribution called reciprocity refers to the exchange of goods and services _____.
   a. of unequal value.
   b. between persons in hierarchical relationships.
   c. for the purpose of maintaining social relationships and gaining prestige.
   d. to make a profit.
   e. to embarrass the person who gave the least.

10. A Navaho gives ten of his sheep that he knows are infected with disease to a Hopi in exchange for a jeep. This is an example of _____.
    a. generalized reciprocity.
    b. balanced reciprocity.
    c. negative reciprocity.
    d. silent trade.
    e. redistribution.

11. The Kula ring _____.
    a. is a marriage ring made of shells.
    b. is found among the Ju/'hoansi.
    c. is found among the Andaman Islanders.
    d. is a circular trade route along which various goods flow.
    e. is a form of silent trade.

12. The American system of paying income taxes every April is an example of _____.
    a. generalized reciprocity.
    b. balanced reciprocity.
    c. negative reciprocity.
    d. redistribution.
    e. market exchange.

13. The display of wealth for social prestige is called _____.
    a. a leveling mechanism.
    b. conspicuous consumption.
    c. redistribution.
    d. balanced reciprocity.
    e. barter.

14. Formal market exchange is usually associated with _____.
    a. hunting and gathering bands.
    b. horticultural tribes.
    c. pastoral tribes.
    d. a state type of political organization.
    e. the household as the unit of production and consumption.

15. A businessperson who wants to build a factory in the Middle East could benefit from the contributions of a cultural anthropologist. In which of the following ways would an anthropologist be likely to help?
    a. provide knowledge of the principles of market exchange
    b. introduce a new method of paying local workers
    c. tell the businessperson how to sit, dress, and talk when making the arrangements with local people
    d. screen workers who have diseases
    e. *b* and *c*

16. An example of tribal leadership is the _____. Such men are leaders of a localized descent groups or of a territorial group.
    a. manager
    b. Big Man
    c. mayor
    d. shaman
    e. chairman

17. The group discussed in the article *Prestige Economics in Papua New Guinea*, was the _____.
    a. Kaluli.
    b. Kapauku.
    c. Enga.
    d. Mekranoti.
    e. Mende.

18. Not only have anthropologists found niches for themselves in the world of business, but since 1972, the number of them going into business has grown _____.
    a. tenfold.
    b. fivefold.
    c. 50 percent.
    d. anthropologists don't work in the business world.
    e. 25 percent.

19. One of the newest innovations in the market-research and design industry is _____.
    a. survey questionnaire.
    b. telephone surveys.
    c. ethnology.
    d. ethnography.
    e. case studies.

20. In the original study "Prestige Economics in Papua New Guinea," it is stated that for Big Man feasts a surplus is created for the express purpose of gaining prestige through a display of wealth and generous giving of gifts-hence the term _____.

    a. surplus economy.
    b. status economy.
    c. festival economy.
    d. prestige economy.
    e. conspicuous consumption.

21. One successful anthropologist working in corporate America doing international consulting for a large computer firm is _____.
    a. Vicki Cassman.
    b. Jennifer Thompson.
    c. Dureen Hughes.
    d. Laura Nader.
    e. Kathleen Gonzales.

22. Not only have anthropologists found niches for themselves in the world of business, but since 1972, the number of them going into business has grown _____.

    a. twofold.
    b. fourfold.
    c. tenfold.
    d. fivefold.
    e. sevenfold.

23. An anthropologist interested in the systems of production, exchange, and redistribution would be called a _____ anthropologist.
    a. political
    b. linguistic
    c. economic
    d. physical
    e. psychological

24. The sexual division of labor configuration that has been described as the flexible/integrated pattern is found among which of the following?
    a. Bakhtiari
    b. Ju/'hoansi
    c. Taiwanese
    d. Dahomeans
    e. Industrial countries

25. One example of specialization is afforded by the _____ people of Ethiopia's Danakil Depression. The men of this group are miners of salt.
    a. Nuer
    b. Azande
    c. Hadza
    d. Afar
    e. Ashanti

26. A societal obligation compelling a family to distribute goods so that no one accumulates more wealth than anyone else is referred to by anthropologists as a

    _____.
    a. flat tax.
    b. commune.
    c. capital gains tax.
    d. poverty spreader.
    e. leveling mechanism.

27. In economic anthropology, a mode of exchange in which the value of the gift is not calculated, nor is the time of repayment specified is known as _____.
    a. charity.
    b. generosity.
    c. a handout.
    d. generalized reciprocity.
    e. Christmas.

28. In political fund-raising in the United States large contributors expect that their "generosity" will buy influence with a candidate. What category of reciprocity would this fall under?
    a. derisive
    b. negative
    c. general
    d. balanced
    e. None of the above

29. Not all trade is motivated by economic considerations. A classic case of this is

    _____.
    a. silent trade.
    b. the swap meet.
    c. the flea market.
    d. the Kula ring.
    e. the *cargo* system.

30. Among the _____, both cacao beans and cotton cloaks served as money.
    a. Tiv
    b. Aztecs
    c. Enga
    d. Trobriand Islanders
    e. Inca

Answers to multiple-choice practice questions

1. b	9. c	17. c	25. d
2. e	10. c	18. b	26. e
3. b	11. d	19. d	27. d
4. c	12. d	20. d	28. d
5. b	13. b	21. c	29. d
6. a	14. d	22. d	30. b
7. b	15. e	23. c	
8. c	16. b	24. b	

True/False Practice Questions

1. _____ According to Robert Lowie, patterns of reciprocity among the Crow did not involve women.

2. _____ In "silent trade," no words are spoken, but the participants must meet face to face to exchange goods.

3. _____ The Inca empire of Peru featured a highly efficient redistributive system.

4. _____ The economist responsible for the concept of "conspicuous consumption" was Thorsten Veblen.

5. _____ The Enga live in Indonesia.

6. _____ Jomo Kenyatta was an anthropologist who became "the father" of modern Kenya.

7. _____ The Big Man feasts exist merely as arenas for grandiose men to flaunt their ambition.

8. _____ Big Man feasts are like conspicuous consumption in Western societies; the emphasis is on the hoarding of goods which would make them unavailable to others.

9. _____ Anthropologists only work in exotic, faraway places like remote islands, deep forests, hostile deserts, or arctic wastelands.

10. _____ There is a potential job market for anthropologists in the market-research and design area.

11. _____ According to your textbook, most anthropologists who work at market-research and design companies are not really "doing ethnography."

12. _____ Doing research in corporate America is not so different from doing initial anthropological research in an unfamiliar culture.

13. _____ Trobriand Island men devote a great deal of time and energy to raise yams, not for themselves but to give to others.

14. _____ No specialization of labor craft exists in nonindustrial societies.

15. _____ Anthropologists have found no form of conspicuous consumption occurring in nonindustrial societies.

16. _____ In non-Western societies the market is an important focus of social as well as economic activity.

17. _____ In Africa, much of the farming is the job of women. Failure to accept this fact is responsible for the failure of many development schemes, since outside experts design projects that usually assume the men in society are the farmers.

Answers to true/false practice questions

1. F	6. T	11. T	16. T
2. F	7. F	12. T	17. T
3. T	8. F	13. T	
4. T	9. F	14. F	
5. F	10. T	15. F	

Practice Essays

1. Compare and contrast the different ideas about the nature and control of land that exist among food foragers, horticulturalists, pastoralists, intensive agriculturalists, and industrialists.

2. Compare and contrast the different ideas about tools and tool ownership in foraging, horticultural, and intensive agricultural societies..

3. Describe the ecological context of the "Big Man" system of the Enga.

4. Describe the prestige economies of the Enga. Explain their function and purpose.

5. Describe what an anthropologist can contribute to the world of business.

6. Compare and contrast a prestige economy with an economy based on conspicuous consumption.

7. Specify and elaborate on the three categories of distribution of material goods as classified by economist Karl Polanyi.

8. What is a "Big Man?" What role does he play in the prestige economies of Melanesia?

Chapter 8
Sex and Marriage

Synopsis

Chapter 8 defines marriage as a system for regulating sexual access and explores the variations on the theme of marriage throughout the world. The interactions of marriage, social structure, and environment are considered.

What You Should Learn from This Chapter

1. Understand what marriage is in nonethnocentric terms.

2. Know the controls societies place on sexual relations and theories as to why these controls are necessary.

3. Understand the many forms of marriage and how they relate with other aspects of society:
   - monogamy
   - polygyny
   - polyandry
   - two forms of cousin marriage

4. Understand the role of consanguineal and affinal ties in society.

5. Know the kinds of gift exchanges that often accompany marriage.

Key Terms and Names

affinal kin

bride price

bride service

Claude Levi-Strauss

conjugal bond

consanguine family

consanguineal kin

dowry

endogamy

exogamy

family

group marriage

incest taboo

levirate

marriage

matrilateral cross-cousin marriage

monogamy

nuclear family

patrilateral parallel-cousin marriage

polyandry

polygyny

serial monogamy

sororate

Review Questions

1. Why are human females able to engage in sexual activity regardless of their ovulation cycles?

2. Why does sexual activity require social control?

3. Describe the sex life of the Trobrianders.

4. As discussed in your textbook, describe the traditional marriage system of the Nayar.

5. What is the incest taboo?

6. Why do people who live in close proximity to one another exhibit reduced sexual activity?

7. What are the Oedipus and Electra complexes?

8. How have geneticists attempted to explain the incest taboo?

9. Distinguish between endogamy and exogamy.

10. What were the initial reasons for exogamy, according to Tylor, Levi-Strauss, and Cohen?

11. Distinguish between marriage and mating.

12. To what extent can North American society be characterized as monogamous?

13. Provide a nonethnocentric definition of marriage.

14. Distinguish between consanguineal and conjugal families.

15. Distinguish between polygynous and polyandrous families.

16. What form of marriage does the majority of the world's societies exhibit?

17. Characterize the typical polygynous society.

18. What is the attitude of Kapauku women towards their husbands' other wives?

19. Describe the social and economic context of polyandry.

20. Discuss the contexts in which sororate, levirate, and serial monogamy are likely to occur.

21. What benefits do arranged marriages have?

22. Describe the marriage system of Sidi Embarek, Morocco.

23. Distinguish between patrilineal parallel-cousin and matrilineal cross-cousin marriage.

24. How is marriage exchange conducted among the Trobrianders?

25. Distinguish between bride price, dowry, and bride service.

26. What is the function of female-female marriage among the Nandi?

27. What role can anthropologists play in the study of AIDS?

Fill-in-the-Blank

1. Marriage is a cultural transaction that regulates men's and women's rights of _____ access to one another and defines the context in which women are eligible to bear children.

2. The female ability to engage is sexual relations at any time is related to the development of _____ locomotion among the hominines.

3. Only about _____ percent of the world's societies prohibit all sexual involvement outside of marriage.

4. The bond between two individuals joined by marriage is called a(n) _____ bond.

5. Households composed only of "blood" relatives are said to contain _____ kin.

6. The _____ taboo prohibits sexual relations between specified individuals.

7. _____ is a rule mandating the one marry outside of a particular group, while _____ mandates marriage within the group.

8. In the United States, _____ is the only legally recognized form of marriage, but some Americans do engage in other forms.

9. A _____ family contains a husband and his multiple wives, while a _____ family contains a wife and her multiple husbands.

10. Among the Turkana of northern Kenya, _____ is the preferred form of marriage.

11. When the wives in a polygynous marriage are sisters, this is called _____ polygyny.

12. _____ marriage refers to a marriage in which several men and women have sexual access to one another.

13. In a _____, a widow marries the brother of her deceased husband; in a _____, a widower marries the sister of his deceased wife.

14. Marrying a sequence of partners throughout one's life is called _____.

15. In a patrilateral parallel-cousin marriage, a boy marries his father's _____ daughter.

16. _____ is a gift exchange occurring at marriage in which money or goods are transferred from the groom's side to the bride's.

17. In a _____ system, the bride's family provides money or goods at the time of marriage.

18. The Nandi of western Kenya practice a form of marriage in which a woman marries _____.

19. Divorce rates in Western society are considered high by many people but are low compared to divorce rates among _____ societies.

20. _____ is a French anthropologist who launched a school of thought called structuralism.

21. Medical anthropologists can contribute significantly to the study of _____ through investigating the social and sexual contexts of disease transmission in various societies.

Exercises

I. Draw your family tree in the space below. Make it as extensive as you can without consulting any of your relatives. What accounts for the relatively truncated kindreds of most North Americans?

II. Briefly identify and locate the following cultures on the map.

1. Nayar

3. Morocco

2. Nandi

4. Tibet

Multiple-Choice Practice Questions

1. _____ is a transaction in which a woman and man establish a continuing claim to the right of sexual access to one another, and in which the woman involved becomes eligible to bear children.
   a. Family
   b. Marriage
   c. Incest
   d. Affinity
   e. Sex

2. One explanation for the tendency of human females to be sexually receptive on a continuing basis is that _____.
   a. it is an accidental byproduct of the high hormone requirements for persistent bipedal locomotion.
   b. it increases competitiveness among the males of a group.
   c. it encourages endogamy.
   d. it discourages incest.
   e. it leads to greater competitiveness among women.

3. Marriage resolves the problem of how to bring sexual activity under _____ control.
   a. biological
   b. male
   c. cultural
   d. female
   e. mother-in-law

4. A household composed of married people contains _____ kin.
   a. affinal
   b. consanguineal
   c. endogamous
   d. nuclear
   e. instinctive

5. According to the _____ theory of incest taboo, children feel so guilty about their sexual feelings for a parent that they repress them, and this is expressed culturally in the incest taboo.
   a. genetic
   b. instinctive
   c. psychological
   d. anthropological
   e. sociological

6. Although all societies have some kind of incest taboo, the relationship that is considered incestuous may vary. Concepts of incest seem to be related to a group's definitions of endogamy and exogamy, thus suggesting that incest taboos may help to promote _____.
   a. alliances between groups.
   b. inbreeding.
   c. brother-sister marriages.
   d. parallel-cousin marriages.
   e. cross-cousin marriages.

7. Marriage within a particular group of individuals is called _____.
   a. incest.
   b. exogamy.
   c. monogamy.
   d. endogamy.
   e. polygamy.

8. The French anthropologist Claude Levi-Strauss says that the incest taboo is universal because humans _____.
   a. are instinctively opposed to inbreeding.
   b. repress their sexual desire for the parent of the opposite sex.
   c. have learned to establish alliances with strangers and thereby share and develop culture.
   d. prefer to marry their brothers and sisters.
   e. don't like sex.

9. A residential kin group composed of a woman, her dependent children, and at least one adult male joined through marriage or blood relationship is a/an _____.
   a. family.
   b. conjugal bond.
   c. endogamous.
   d. nuclear family.
   e. serial marriage.

10. Families can be consanguineal or conjugal. The conjugal family has many forms. One type of conjugal family is the _____, consisting of the husband, wife, and dependent children.
    a. polygynous family
    b. polygamous family
    c. polyandrous family
    d. nuclear family
    e. extended family

11. Although _____ may statistically be the most common form of marriage
    around the world, it is not the most preferred.
    a. polygyny
    b. monogamy
    c. polyandry
    d. polygamy
    e. the levirate

12. Polygyny _____.
    a. means marriage to more than one man.
    b. is the most common form of marriage.
    c. is usually possible only when a man is fairly wealthy.
    d. is less common than polyandry.
    e. is an example of group marriage.

13. An example of group marriage would be _____.
    a. a pastoral nomad's wife among the Turkana who actively searches for another
       woman to share her husband and her work with the livestock.
    b. the Moonies having a large wedding ceremony at which five hundred couples,
       each one assigned to another, are married at the same time.
    c. a prosperous member of the Kapauku in western New Guinea who is able to
       afford a bride price for four wives.
    d. a hippy commune in the Haight-Ashbury district in which it is accepted that all
       adult members of the commune have sexual access to each other.
    e. a Nayar household in which a woman takes several lovers.

14. The levirate and the sororate _____.
    a. are secret societies, like sororities and fraternities.
    b. function to maintain the relationship between the family of the bride and the
       family of the groom.
    c. are *usually* possible only when the man is fairly wealthy
    d. are types of cattle in pastoralist societies.
    e. exist only in advanced industrial societies.

15. Serial monogamy tends to occur in societies where _____.
    a. a woman with children receives a great deal of help from her mother and brothers.
    b. women do not have many children.
    c. a woman with dependent children, isolated from her parents, marries a series of
       partners to get the assistance of another adult.
    d. women are very wealthy.
    e. divorce is forbidden.

16. The main function of a bride price is _____.
    a. for a man to show off to his wife how rich he is.
    b. for a man to buy a slave.
    c. for the wife's people to gain prestige in the village.
    d. to compensate the wife's family for her labor.
    e. for the wife's people to buy a husband for their daughter.

17. When a man marries his father's brother's daughter in ancient Greece or traditional China,
    a. he is committing incest.
    b. he is practicing matrilineal cross-cousin marriage.
    c. he is practicing patrilateral parallel-cousin marriage.
    d. he is keeping property within the single male line of descent.
    e. *c* and *d*

18. In which of the following situations would you expect to find the custom of bride price?
    a. A bride and groom leave the community after marriage and set up their own household in a distant city.
    b. A bride and groom go to live with the bride's people.
    c. A bride and groom go to live with the groom's people.
    d. A bride and groom go to live with the bride's mother's brother.
    e. none of the above

19. When the economy is based on _____ and where the man does most of the productive work, the bride's people may give a dowry that protects the woman against desertion and is a statement of her economic status.
    a. food foraging
    b. pastoralism
    c. intensive agriculture
    d. horticulture
    e. industrialism

20. The woman/woman marriage custom found in sub-Saharan Africa _____.
    a. enables a woman without sons to inherit a share of her husband's property.
    b. confers legitimacy on the children of a woman who had been unable to find a husband.
    c. enables the woman who adopts a male identity to raise her status.
    d. enables the woman who is the wife of the female husband to raise her status and live a more secure life.
    e. all of the above

21. Which of the following constitutes a culturally valid reason for divorce among different groups?
    a. sterility or impotence
    b. cruelty
    c. being a poor provider
    d. being a lazy housekeeper
    e. all of the above

22. In an arranged marriage in India, the newly married couple will go to live in a _____ family.
    a. nuclear
    b. combined
    c. mixed
    d. joint
    e. consanguine

23. According to the article in your textbook "Arranging Marriage in India," among urban Indians an important source of contacts in trying to arrange a marriage is/are the _____.
    a. social club.
    b. newspaper personals.
    c. internet chat rooms.
    d. match making businesses.
    e. temple.

24. Which of the following characteristics would be most important in an Indian family's selection of a bride for their son?
    a. good looks
    b. well-educated
    c. independent
    d. have higher social status
    e. good character

25. _____ is the leading exponent of French structuralism.
    a. Bronislaw Malinowski
    b. Franz Boas
    c. Claude Levi-Strauss
    d. Phillipe Cousteau
    e. Emile Durkiem

26. What sets _____ apart is that sex may occur even when the female is not swollen.
    a. chimpanzees
    b. bonobos
    c. macaques
    d. orangutangs
    e. gorillas

27. According to Haviland, in the United States there are somewhere between 20,000 and _____ people in the Rocky Mountain states that live in households made up of a man with two or more wives.
    a. 100,000
    b. 75,000
    c. 15,000
    d. 1 million
    e. 60,000

28. In _____, the state legislature recently passed, and the governor signed, a bill that permits same-sex partners to enjoy all the benefits of marriage.
    a. California
    b. Delaware
    c. New Hampshire
    d. Massachusetts
    e. Vermont

29. No societies have achieved greater separation between the sexual and reproductive attributes of women than the _____.
    a. Nandi.
    b. Nayar.
    c. Azande.
    d. Mundugamor.
    e. the United States and other Western countries.

30. _____ saw exogamy as the basis of a distinction between early hominine life isolated endogamous groups and the of *Homo sapiens* in a supportive society with an accumulating culture.
    a. R.M. Keesing
    b. Claude Levi-Strauss
    c. Yehudi Cohen
    d. Edward Sapir
    e. Clyde Kluckhohn

31. In the United States, as in most Western countries, _____ is the only legally recognized form of marriage.
    a. polygamy
    b. polygyny
    c. monogamy
    d. polyandry
    e. serial

32. Most divorced people in the United States remarry at least once. Thus, _____ is not uncommon.
    a. polygamy
    b. serial monogamy
    c. sororate marriage
    d. levirate marriage
    e. polyandry

33. Conjugal families are formed on the basis of marital ties between husband and wife. Which of the following are forms of conjugal families?
    a. polyandrous families
    b. consanguine families
    c. polygynous families
    d. nuclear families
    e. all but *b*

34. In some societies when a woman marries she receives her share of the family inheritance, or her _____.
    a. bride price.
    b. bride service.
    c. dowry.
    d. bride commission.
    e. birthright.

35. Among the _____ of Kenya, sterility or impotence were grounds for divorce.
    a. Eritreans
    b. Gusii
    c. Nandi
    d. Hutu
    e. Chenchu

36. In some societies, preferred marriages are a man marrying his father's brother's daughter. This is known as patrilateral parallel-cousin marriage. Although not obligatory, such marriages have been favored historically among which of the following cultures?
    a. traditional Chinese
    b. Arabs
    c. ancient Greece
    d. ancient Israelites
    e. all of the above

Answers to multiple-choice practice questions

1. b	10. d	19. c	28. e
2. a	11. b	20. e	29. e
3. c	12. c	21. e	30. b
4. a	13. d	22. d	31. c
5. c	14. b	23. a	32. b
6. a	15. c	24. e	33. e
7. d	16. d	25. c	34. c
8. c	17. e	26. b	35. b
9. a	18. c	27. e	36. e

True/False Practice Questions

1. _____ Trobriand children begin sexual experimentation at a young age.

2. _____ About half of the world's societies prohibit sexual involvement outside of marriage.

3. _____ Haviland believes that evidence on intrafamily homicides support Freud's theories of the Oedipus and Electra complex.

4. _____ Brother-sister marriages were common among farmers in Roman Egypt.

5. _____ Primate evidence shows that it is likely that humans started out as a monogamous species.

6. _____ People want pretty much the same things in marriage whether it is in India or America.

7. _____ Today, a dowry is expected by law in India.

8. _____ In India it is understood that matches (marriages) would be arranged only within the same caste and general social class.

9. _____ In India no crossing of subcastes is permissible even if the class positions of the bride's and groom's families are similar.

10. _____ As far as arranging a marriage is concerned, in India the basic rule seems to be that a family's reputation is most important.

11. _____ Although it is common for the newly married Indian couple to go live with the groom's joint family in the rural area, it is not common among the urban, upper-middle class in India.

12. _____ In India divorce is still a scandal and thus the divorce rate is exceedingly low.

13. _____ When arranging an Indian marriage consideration of a girl's looks are more important than her character.

14. _____ In an arranged marriage in India a woman is being judged as a prospective daughter- in-law as much as a prospective bride.

15. _____ In an arranged Indian marriage, offering the proper gifts is often an important factor in influencing the relationship between the bride's and groom's families, and the treatment of the bride in her new home.

16. _____ In India a military career with its economic security has great prestige and is considered a benefit in finding a suitable bride.

17. _____ While a boy's skin color is a less important consideration than a girl's, it is still a factor when arranging a marriage in India.

18. _____ Bonobos will not engage in sex when a female is pregnant.

19. _____ Both cross-cultural studies, and those of other animals, suggest that homosexual behavior is unnatural.

20. _____ In a number of societies researchers have discovered that same-sex marriages are regarded as perfectly appropriate.

21. _____ Among primates, in general, monogamous mating patterns are not common.

22. _____ In the United States today, single-parent households outnumber nuclear family households.

23. _____ The obsession with a particular idea of feminine beauty in the United States is reflected in the beauty pageants organized for very young girls.

24. _____ Divorce is possible in all societies, though reasons for divorce as well as its frequency vary widely from one society to another.

Answers to true/false practice questions

1. T	7. F	13. F	19. F
2. F	8. T	14. T	20. T
3. F	9. F	15. T	21. T
4. T	10. T	16. F	22. T
5. F	11. F	17. T	23. T
6. F	12. T	18. F	24. T

Practice Matching

Match the culture with its characteristic.

1. _____Nandi

2. _____Moroccans

3. _____Nayar

4. _____Tibetans

5. _____North Americans

a. A culture emphasizing love and choice as a basis for marriage.
b. South Indian people who give the mother's brothers key responsibility in child rearing.
c. Patrilineal North African people who practice arranged marriage.
d. East African pastoralists who practice woman/woman marriage.
e. Polyandrous society of central Asia.

Answers to practice matching

1. d   2. c   3. b   4. e   5. a

Practice Essays

1. Describe how the "romantic love" complex impacts North American marriage patterns. Is romantic love involved in marriage in India? Discuss why or why not?

2. What factors affect the stability of marriages and the choice of mates?

3. What factors must be taken into consideration when arranging a marriage in India? Describe.

4. Describe the contributions of anthropologists to our understanding and control of AIDS.

5. Describe the Nayar and their rules of sexual access.

6. Anthropologists have found that universally societies have cultural rules that act to control sexual relations. What are the rules of sexual access from one culture to another?

7. What is the "incest taboo?" Explain why is it such a challenge for anthropologists to explain in terms of its universality and why incest commonly should be regarded as such loathsome behavior?

8. Explain the distinction between marriage and mating.

9. Discuss the arrangement of marriage in India.

10. Expound on the reasons and frequency of divorce from society to society.

Chapter 9
Family and Household

Synopsis

Chapter 9 focuses on the differences between families and households, noting that the Western assumption that all households are built around conjugal relationships is ethnocentric. The major residence patterns are defined, and the various problems created by different kinds of living arrangements are explored.

What You Should Learn from This Chapter

1. Understand the functions of the family in human society and the difference between family and household.

2. Know the various forms of family organization and the difficulties associated with each:
   • polygynous
   • extended
   • nuclear
   • female-headed

3. Know the basic kinds of residence rules that are found in diverse societies:
   • patrilocal
   • matrilocal
   • ambilocal
   • neolocal
   • avunculocal

Key Terms

ambilocal residence

avunculocal residence

conjugal family

extended family

household

matrilocal residence

neolocal residence

patrilocal residence

Review Questions

1. How does Haviland define "family?"

2. How did historical and social circumstances shape the character of the Western family?

3. Describe the care and nurturance of the young among primates.

4. Describe the various ways in which households can be structured.

5. How is the modern American family related to the rise of industrial capitalism?

6. Describe the nuclear family.

7. What relations might be a part of the extended family?

8. What societal factors might contribute to the existence of extended families?

9. Distinguish the five common patterns of residence.

10. How does ecology impact residence pattern?

11. What residence pattern was traditionally followed by people along the Maine coast and why?

12. What residence pattern was traditionally followed by the Hopi and how did it influence family life?

13. What problems may accompany polygynous families and how are they handled?

14. What problems may accompany extended families and how are they resolved?

15. What problems may accompany nuclear families and how are they worked out?

16. What problems may accompany female-headed families and how are they dealt with?

17. Why did the patriarchal colonial family fade away over time?

18. How does the status of women relate to various kinds of family and residence patterns?

Fill-in-the-Blank

1. The independent nuclear family emerged in Europe in the fourth century A.D. in response to regulations put forward by _____.

2. The "ever-changing family in North America" was studied by _____.

3. A family based on a marital tie is called a _____ family, while a family based on blood ties is called a _____ family.

4. A _____ is a residential group composed of a woman, her dependent children, and at least one male joined through marriage or a blood relationship.

5. Among the Mundurucu, after age thirteen boys go to live in _____.

6. Two examples of the rare consanguineal family are the _____ and the _____.

7. Two examples of societies based on independent nuclear families are the _____ and the _____.

8. In a _____ form of residence, husbands go to live with their wife's parents after marriage.

9. In a _____ form of residence, wives go to live with their husband's parents after marriage.

10. The Hopi practice _____ residence while the Chinese practice _____ residence.

11. Among the Trobrianders, a newly married couple goes to live with the groom's mother's brother. This is called _____ residence.

12. The Mbuti practice _____ residence.

13. During colonial times _____ children were treated much like servants, especially if they were of the same or similar age.

Exercises

I. Anthropologists have developed a method of expressing kin relationships symbolically. In this form of notation, males are represented by triangles and females by circles. A bond of marriage is represented by an equal sign (two parallel lines) while a consanguineal bond is represented by a single line. For example, the following diagram shows a conventional nuclear family of a husband, wife, and two children:

There are further specifications possible in the standard genealogical notation. If an individual is deceased, he or she is represented by a diagonal line drawn through the triangle or circle. Here is a diagram of a widow with her three sons and one daughter. In the society in which this hypothetical family lives, goods are inherited through the female line, from mother to daughter. This is indicated on the diagram by coloring in the triangles and circles in the line of inheritance (the lineage).

Sometimes other kinds of modifications can be added to a genealogical chart as well. For example, a residence group might be indicated by drawing a line around the individuals included in the household. The following shows an extended family household based on ties between brothers.

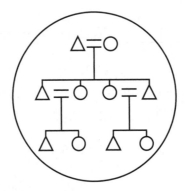

Now redraw your family tree from Chapter 8 using standard genealogical notation. (Don't worry about inheritance or residence here; just diagram the basic affinal and consanguineal ties).

II. On the three charts below, illustrate a ***patrilocal*** residence group, a ***matrilocal***
residence group, and an ***avunculocal*** residence group by drawing a line around the
included individuals.

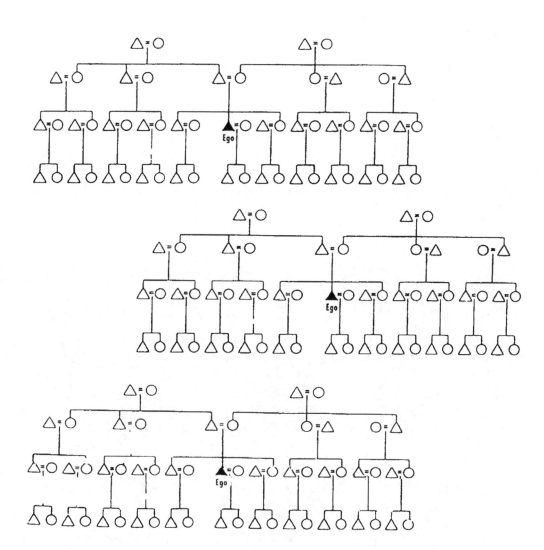

III. Briefly identify and locate the following cultures:

1. Mundurucu   4. Inuit

2. Tory Islanders   5. Hopi

3. Coastal Mainers

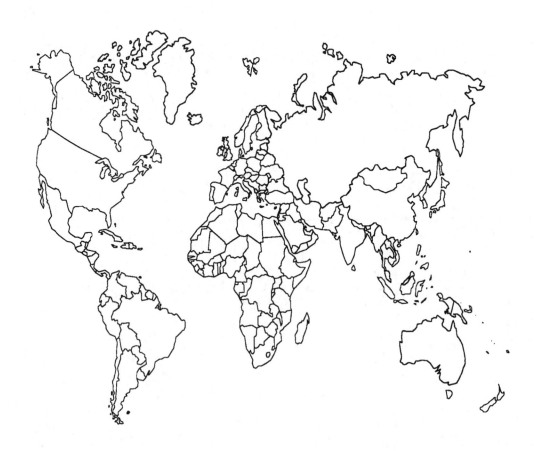

Multiple-Choice Practice Questions

1. The independent nuclear family in Europe _____.
   a. emerged recently as the result of regulations passed by the Roman Catholic Church in the fourth century A.D.
   b. is a universal family form that is natural to primates.
   c. is found only in Europe and places to which Europeans have emigrated.
   d. is found only in non-Western societies.
   e. was the only form of family considered legitimate in the Old Testament of the Bible.

2. The effect of industrialization on nuclear families was _____.
   a. an increased dependence on extended kin, who could provide aid during difficult times.
   b. greater isolation because of the mobility required of an industrial labor force.
   c. greater conflict among members of the nuclear family over scarce jobs.
   d. the tendency to develop polygyny.
   e. the tendency to develop the levirate.

3. Which of the following statements is **correct**?
   a. The period of infant dependency in humans is the same as that in other primates.
   b. The family is the only unit in which children can be reared in a nurturant manner.
   c. Only among humans are males larger and stronger than females.
   d. Human infants can survive only with the care provided by the biological mother.
   e. none of the above

4. A household is _____.
   a. a residential group composed of a woman, her dependent children, and at least one male.
   b. joined through marriage or consanguineal relationship.
   c. a nonresidential group composed of people who share common interests.
   d. a residential unit within which economic production, consumption, inheritance, child rearing and shelter are organized and carried out.
   e. a temporary association of strangers.
   f. a research center.

5. A residential kin group composed of related women, their brothers, and the women's offspring is _____.
   a. a conjugal family.
   b. an extended family.
   c. a consanguineal family.
   d. a nuclear family.
   e. a patrilocal family.

6. What do traditional Inuit society and contemporary North American society have in common that explains the similarity in their family structure?
   a. Both developed in arctic environments.
   b. Both rely on the technology of hunting.
   c. In both, people have very few possessions so there is little jealousy.
   d. Both care for their elderly.
   e. Both are highly mobile.

7. The _____ is composed of people related to each other by ties of blood who bring their spouses to live in the family.
   a. extended family
   b. polygamous family
   c. consanguine family
   d. nuclear family
   e. communal family

8. Residence patterns refer to _____.
   a. how a group makes its living in a particular environment.
   b. the structure of a family under certain ecological conditions.
   c. where a couple chooses to live after they are married.
   d. the problems that different families have.
   e. whether the husband and wife sleep in the same room or in different rooms after they are married.

9. Societies that rely on animal husbandry or intensive agriculture, in which polygyny is customary and where warfare is prominent enough to make male cooperation important, are most likely to practice _____ residence.
   a. matrilocal
   b. avunculocal
   c. ambilocal
   d. patrilocal
   e. neolocal

10. Ambilocal residence is found in societies _____.
    a. that stress the cooperation of women.
    b. where warfare is common and men wield authority.
    c. where economic activity occurs outside the family, and families have to move frequently in search of jobs.
    d. where males control property but descent and inheritance are reckoned through women.
    e. where the nuclear family is not sufficient to handle the economic activities required for the family's survival, but resources are limited.

11. Neolocal residence is common in industrial societies like our own because

    _____.
    a. newlyweds do not usually get along with their in-laws.
    b. industries require workers to be able to move to wherever there are jobs.
    c. most families set up their own businesses, and they do not require the labor of other family members outside the nuclear family.
    d. brothers need to stay together for purposes of conducting warfare.
    e. women continue to live with their brothers after marriage.

12. Which of the following statements about residence patterns in the Trobriand Islands is **incorrect**?
    a. All couples live with the husband's mother's brother.
    b. Men who are in line to take over control of their descent group's assets will take their wives to live with their mother's brother.
    c. Most couples live patrilocally.
    d. Men who live with their fathers gain access to land controlled by their fathers' descent groups.
    e. Men who live with their fathers also have access to land controlled through female descent.

13. A man who marries several sisters is practicing _____.
    a. avunculocal residence.
    b. sororal polygyny.
    c. fraternal polyandry.
    d. infidelity.
    e. matrilocal residence.

14. Extended families usually work more effectively if authority is in the hands of one person, such as the eldest son. Which of the following methods of reducing conflict between this eldest son and his younger brothers are likely to be found in extended families?
    a. moving out of the household
    b. dependence training
    c. independence training
    d. increasing the number of wives for the younger sons
    e. murder of the eldest son

15. Extended families have which of the following problems?
    a. loneliness caused by isolation from kin
    b. Children are raised to be independent, which competes with group harmony.
    c. The eldest son is in competition with his younger brothers for the position of authority in the household.
    d. The mothers-in-law are powerless.
    e. The mother's brother is the authority figure.

16. What are some of the problems associated with the nuclear family?
    a. Husbands and wives tend to be isolated from their kin.
    b. There are no clear-cut lines of authority and rules for making decisions.
    c. The elderly cannot depend on their children for aid when they are too old to take care of themselves.
    d. There is very little privacy.
    e. all but *d*

17. The increase in number of single-parent households headed by women is likely to be associated with _____.
    a. increased child support being paid by fathers.
    b. increased participation of extended kin in caring for the children.
    c. increased number of women below the poverty line.
    d. decreased number of welfare programs.
    e. decreased number of women below the poverty line in third-world countries.

18. In the original 13 colonies people lived in households, each typically consisting of _____.
    a. an extended family.
    b. a nuclear family.
    c. the mother's brother's family.
    d. the father's sister's family.
    e. a clan.

19. In her book on the history of American families, _____ wrote that "The central room or hall was where work, meals, play, religious instruction, and often sleep took place...."
    a. Coontz
    b. Galloway
    c. Cott
    d. Mead
    e. Benedict

20. Single parent households headed by women have been known and studied for a long time in the _____.
    a. countries of southern Europe.
    b. country of India.
    c. countries of Central America.
    d. countries of the Caribbean basin.
    e. countries of sub-Saharan Africa.

21. In colonial North America people freely intruded into one another's households, and the affairs of all were carefully monitored and regulated by which of the following?
    a. village officials
    b. family members
    c. friends of the family
    d. church officials
    e. *a* and *d*

22. Colonial women were clearly subordinate, but a colonial woman's subordination was seen as a social necessity, **not** as a unique female condition caused by her

    _____.
    a. enculturation.
    b. assimilation.
    c. biology.
    d. culture.
    e. natural passivity.

23. In some areas of colonial North America, such as the South (U.S.) and New France (Quebec), _____ marriage was practiced in order to consolidate land and transmit wealth in family lines.
    a. cousin
    b. sibling
    c. common-law
    d. same-sex
    e. arranged

24. As the patriarchal colonial family faded away, there was a general trend toward increasing _____.
    a. wealth.
    b. privacy.
    c. openness.
    d. equality.
    e. immorality.

25. During the late 18th and early 19th centuries, a middle-class woman went to work outside the home for which of the following reasons?
    a. widowhood
    b. unemployment of the husband
    c. to purchase desired items
    d. to help with family expenses
    e. *a* and *b*

26. Which of the following did **not** occur to the population of the United States after the end of World War II?
    a. the age of marriage dropped
    b. fertility rose
    c. divorce declined
    d. the middle class moved to the suburbs
    e. women's participation in the work force decreased

27. From the early 1970s to the late 1990s, the percentage of children living with single parents rose from 4.7 percent to _____ percent.
    a. 18.2
    b. 25
    c. 50
    d. 10.4
    e. 15.5

28. The nuclear family, consisting of a married family and dependent children, is held up as the ideal in the United States. However, only _____ percent of U.S. households now conform to the independent nuclear family ideal.
    a. 50
    b. 26
    c. 11
    d. 5
    e. 15

29. The form of conjugal family most familiar to most North Americans is the independent nuclear family. This type of family is also apt to be prominent in societies such as the _____ that live in harsh environments.
    a. Bakhtiari
    b. Bantu
    c. Inuit
    d. Mekranoti Kayapo
    e. Gururumba

30. In the United States the extended family still exists in some places like along the
    _____.
    a. the Pacific Northwest coast.
    b. the southern California coast.
    c. the Mississippi River.
    d. the Maine coast.
    e. the shores of Lake Michigan.

31. _____ residence is particularly well suited to situations where economic
    cooperation of more people than available in the nuclear family is needed, but where
    resources are limited in some way.
    a. Patrilocal
    b. Matrilocal
    c. Neolocal
    d. Ambilocal
    e. Avunculocal

32. Which of the following is **not a** circumstance related to the specific form a family
    takes?
    a. social
    b. historical
    c. biological
    d. ecological
    e. none of the above

33. The nuclear family, consisting of a married family and dependent offspring, is held
    up as the ideal in which of the following societies?
    a. Tory Islanders
    b. Nayar
    c. Inuit
    d. United States
    e. *c* and *d*

34. The problems that arise in neolocal families are especially difficult in North
    American society because of which of the following?
    a. inequality that still persists between men and women
    b. the great emphasis placed on individualism and competition
    c. the absence of clearly understood patterns of responsibility between husbands and
       wives
    d. a clear model for child rearing
    e. all of the above

Answers to multiple-choice practice questions

1. a	10. e	19. a	28. b
2. b	11. b	20. d	29. c
3. e	12. a	21. e	30. d
4. c	13. b	22. c	31. d
5. c	14. b	23. a	32. c
6. e	15. c	24. b	33. e
7. a	16. e	25. e	34. e
8. c	17. c	26. e	
9. d	18. b	27. a	

True/False Practice Questions

1. _____ A woman who marries several brothers is practicing sororal polygyny.

2. _____ Neolocal residence is common when the nuclear family must be able to move independently.

3. _____ Among the Mundurucu, the men's houses and the women's houses constitute separate families.

4. _____ Among the Hopi, daughters brought their husbands to live near their mother's house.

5. _____ In an avunculocal residence pattern, the newly married couple goes to live with the bride's father's sister.

6. _____ During colonial times few households contained people who were not kin to one another.

7. _____ Households in colonial America, much like today in some parts of the United States, privacy was of paramount importance.

8. _____ Unlike the way "the home" was seen in colonial North America, today in most households, "the home" is seen as a retreat from the stress and strain of the outside world.

9. _____ The colonial household was a center of economic production with no clear division between the public and the private.

10. _____ Colonial women constantly argued for equal status with colonial men.

11. _____ Female headed households are in fact a pathological response to economic restraints in U.S. society.

12. _____ Single parent households headed by women are relatively rare and are restricted to industrialized societies like the United States.

13. _____ Women constitute the majority of the poor, the underprivileged and the economically and socially disadvantaged in most of the world's societies, just as is becoming the case in the U.S.

14. _____ Colonial women did not need to grapple with reasons for their lack of equal status, since equal status was not even a social value for men.

15. _____ The concept of "face" may constitute a particularly potent check on children of extended families.

16. _____ More women than ever in the United States and abroad find themselves much better off than they were a decade ago.

17. _____ In the United States and Canada it is not considered desirable for young people to live with their parents beyond a certain age.

Answers to true/false practice questions

1. F	6. F	11. F	16. F
2. T	7. F	12. F	17. T
3. F	8. T	13. T	
4. T	9. T	14. T	
5. F	10. F	15. F	

Practice Matching

Match the culture with its characteristic.

1. _____Inuit

2. _____Coastal Mainers

3. _____Mundurucu

4. _____Tory Islanders

5. _____Hopi

a. Irish society centered on consanguineal families.

b. Amazon people with "men's houses."

c. Americans maintaining an extended family tradition.

d. Southwestern Native Americans with families headed by women.

e. Arctic people who live in nuclear families.

Answers to practice matching

1. e   2. c   3. b   4. a   5. d

Practice Essays

1. Senator Daniel Patrick Moynihan was the author of a classic study on the problems of urban black people in the United States. Known as "the Moynihan Report," this document blamed irresponsible males and the resultant female-headed families for many of the ills that plague the African-American community. How might an anthropologist respond to this claim? (In fact, an anthropologist did respond to it. Her name is Carol Stack and her book *All Our Kin* was a significant landmark in our understanding of African-American culture. You might like to have a look at both the Moynihan Report and *All Our Kin* to see how anthropological insights can contribute to more appropriate government policies.)

2. Coontz suggests that the ideal American family as portrayed in the television series "Leave it to Beaver" is largely a myth. Explain why she has arrived at that conclusion.

3. Identify and discuss the problems inherent in the "traditional" nuclear family.

4. Discuss why the family today in the United States has become a matter of controversy and concern.

5. Where some form of conjugal or extended family is the norm, family exogamy requires that either the husband or wife, if not both, must move to a new household upon marriage. Describe the five most common patterns of residence open to newlyweds in extended families.

Chapter 10
Kinship and Descent

Synopsis

Chapter 10 presents some key concepts relating to the anthropological study of kinship and descent. The relationship of kinship patterns to other elements of social organization is explored.

What You Should Learn from This Chapter

1. Know the difference between kindreds and lineal descent groups.

2. Understand the various types of descent systems:
   • patrilineal
   • matrilineal
   • double descent
   • ambilineal

3. Understand the organization and function of descent groups:
   • lineage
   • clan
   • phratry
   • moiety

4. Recognize the major systems of kinship terminology:
   • Eskimo
   • Hawaiian
   • Iroquois
   • Crow
   • Omaha
   • Descriptive

Key Terms and Names

ambilineal descent

clan

Crow system

descent group

double descent

Eskimo system

fission

Hawaiian system

Iroquois system

kindred

Lewis Henry Morgan

lineage

matrilineal descent

moiety

Omaha system

patrilineal descent

phratry

Sudanese or descriptive system

totemism

unilineal descent

Review Questions

1. Why do societies form descent groups?

2. How is membership in a descent group restricted?

3. Distinguish between patrilineal and matrilineal descent groups

4. What function does double descent serve in Yako society?

5. Explain the function of ambilineal descent in contemporary North America. Provide an example.

6. What functions do descent groups serve?

7. How is a lineage reckoned?

8. What are the social implications of lineage exogamy?

9. Contrast a clan and a lineage.

10. What did anthropologist Magery Wolf find out about the situation of women in Taiwan?

11. What purpose do totems serve a clan?

12. Distinguish between a phratry and a moiety.

13. How do bilateral systems differ from unilateral systems?

14. What are the functions and limitations of ego-centered groups?

15. Why do descent groups emerge?

16. What functions do kinship terminologies serve?

17. What are the six major systems of kinship terminology?

18. What is the main feature of the Eskimo system of descent?

19. What is the simplest descent system? Why is it considered simple?

20. With which type of descent group is Iroquois terminology commonly correlated?

21. How can anthropologists assist Native Americans in their struggles for federal recognition?

Exercises

I. On the two charts provided below, color in a *matrilineal descent group* and a *patrilineal descent group*.

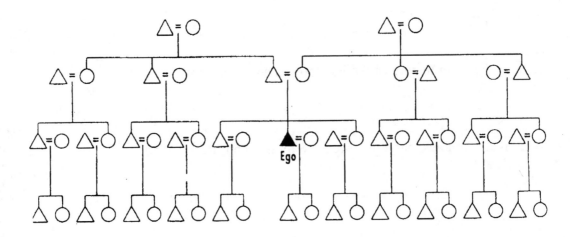

II. What kind of terminological system is shown here?

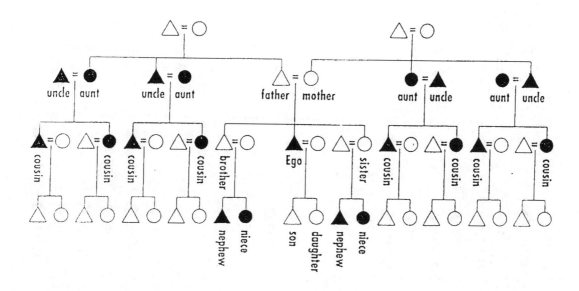

III. What kind of terminological system is shown here?

IV. What kind of terminological system is shown here?

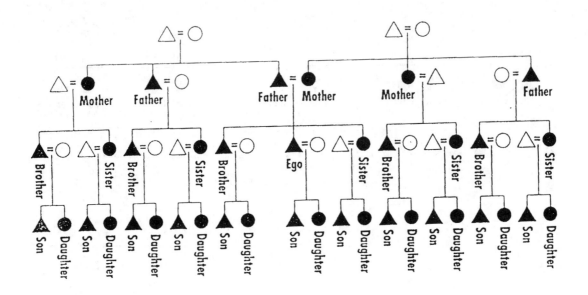

V. In the system below, what should Ego call the individual marked "X"?

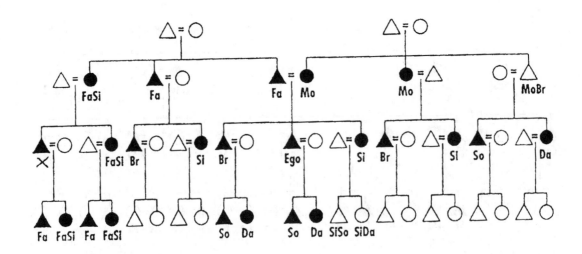

VI. On the chart below, illustrate a descriptive type terminological system.

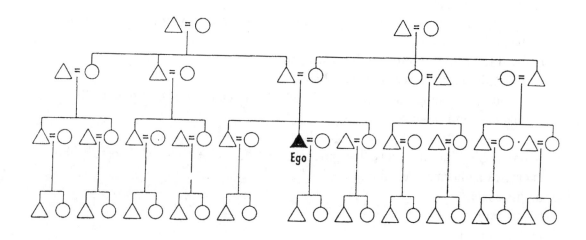

Multiple-Choice Practice Questions

1. Descent groups _____.
   a. are composed of those who claim to be lineally descended from a particular ancestor.
   b. are common in human societies.
   c. trace their connections back to a common ancestor through a chain of parent-child links, and thus appear to stem from the parent-child bond.
   d. help provide jobs for their members.
   e. all but *d*

2. By tracing membership either through males or through females, members of unilineal descent groups _____.
   a. know exactly to which group they belong and where their primary loyalties lie.
   b. are confused about their relationship to persons not included in the group.
   c. act like females if they are in a matrilineal group.
   d. act life males if they are in a patrilineal group.
   e. know exactly how many children they are going to have.

3. You belong to a patrilineal descent group. Which of the following belong to the same group?
   a. your mother
   b. your father's sister
   c. your mother's sister
   d. your mother's father
   e. your father's sister's children

4. The primary way in which a woman in traditional China could exert any influence was
_____.
   a. through her close tie with her husband.
   b. by appealing to her mother-in-law who will intercede with her husband on her behalf.
   c. by threatening to return to her own people.
   d. through the influence of her brothers.
   e. through the village women's gossip which can cause a loss of face for her husband and father-in-law.

5. A boy is born into a society that practices matrilineal descent. The person who exercises authority over him is _____.
   a. his sister.
   b. his father.
   c. his mother.
   d. his mother's brother.
   e. his father's sister.

6. Among the Yako of Nigeria, an individual might inherit grazing lands from his father's patrilineal group, and livestock and ritual knowledge from his mother's matrilineal group. This is an example of _____ descent.
   a. ambilineal
   b. bilocal
   c. patrilateral
   d. indivisible
   e. double

7. A cousins club _____.
   a. is an ambilineal descent group to which younger-generation descendants of east European Jewish immigrants belong.
   b. is a double descent group to which only cross cousins belong.
   c. is a patrilineal descent group composed of the children of Norman Cousins.
   d. is a cognatic descent group composed of women only.
   e. is a unlineal descent group for first and second cousins.

8. Descent groups _____.
   a. are economic units providing mutual aid.
   b. provide social security for elderly members.
   c. often promote solidarity by encouraging worship of the group's ancestors.
   d. play a role in deciding appropriate marriage partners.
   e. all of the above

9. A lineage is a corporate descent group _____.
   a. the members of which can buy shares in the corporation.
   b. the members of which claim descent from a common ancestor.
   c. the members of which know the exact genealogical linkages by which they are related to the common ancestor.
   d. composed of consanguineal kin.
   e. all but *a*

10. A totem _____.
    a. is a word that comes from the Ojibwa American Indian word that means "he is a relative of mine."
    b. is a symbol of animals, plants, natural forces, and objects.
    c. is usually associated with a clan's concept of its mythical origins.
    d. may be found in our own society in the names we give to baseball and football teams.
    e. all of the above

11. A phratry is a unilineal descent group composed of two or more _____ that believe they are related to each other.
    a. moieties
    b. totems
    c. kindred
    d. lineages
    e. clans

12. Members of a moiety _____.
    a. belong to one of two major descent groups in a society.
    b. are those who are divorced (they lack their "better half").
    c. are usually able to trace their exact genealogical links to their common ancestor.
    d. feel a much stronger feeling of kinship than is felt by members of a lineage or clan.
    e. belong to a group that is smaller than a lineage.

13. A person in a system of bilateral descent _____.
    a. traces descent through the father for some purposes, and through the mother for other purposes.
    b. traces descent through female lines.
    c. traces descent through male lines.
    d. uses totems to symbolically represent the group.
    e. traces descent through both parents simultaneously and recognizes multiple ancestors.

14. Descent groups are frequently found to be important organizing devices in
    _____.
    a. food-foraging societies.
    b. horticultural societies.
    c. pastoral societies.
    d. intensive agricultural societies.
    e. all of the above except *a*

15. _____ develop out of extended families when families split up and move
    to nearby regions, and the core members of these families recognize their descent
    from a common ancestor and continue to organize activities based on this idea.
    a. Phratries
    b. Kindred groups
    c. Lineages
    d. Moieties
    e. Cognatic groups

16. If two people are given the same kinship term, this means that _____.
    a. they have the same genes.
    b. no one can tell the difference between them.
    c. they occupy a similar status.
    d. they are identical twins.
    e. they are members of an adopted family.

17. In _____ kinship terminology, ego's "brother" and "sister" are
    distinguished from "cousins"; both ego's father's brother and mother's brother are
    given the same kinship term, "uncle."
    a. Eskimo
    b. Hawaiian
    c. Crow
    d. Omaha
    e. Iroquois

18. In the _____ system of kinship terminology, ego's father, father's
    brother, and mother's brother are all referred to by the same term, and ego's mother,
    mother's sister, and father's sister are all referred to by the same term; the term
    "brother" includes ego's brothers as well as male cousins.
    a. Iroquois
    b. Crow
    c. Omaha
    d. Hawaiian
    e. Eskimo

19. In _____ kinship terminology, the term "brother" is given to ego's brother, father's brother's son, and mother's sister's son; a different term is used for the sons of father's sister and mother's brother. "Mother" refers to ego's mother and mother's sister, "father" refers to ego's father and father's brother. Separate terms are used for ego's mother's brother and father's sister.
    a. Eskimo
    b. Hawaiian
    c. Iroquois
    d. cognatic
    e. kindred

20. The Crow kinship terminology system _____.
    a. is associated with matrilineal descent.
    b. merges paternal cross-cousins with the paternal generation.
    c. is associated with patrilineal descent.
    d. merges maternal cross-cousins with the generation of ego's children.
    e. all but *c*

21. The Omaha kinship terminology system _____.
    a. is associated with partrilineal descent.
    b. merges maternal cross-cousins with the parental generation.
    c. merges paternal cross-cousins with the generation of ego's children.
    d. identifies maternal cross-cousins with the lineage of ego's mother (the lineage that supplies women to ego's patrilineage).
    e. all of the above

22. The descriptive system of kinship terminology _____.
    a. gives the same kinship term for ego's mother's brother and father's brother.
    b. is the most common form of kinship terminology.
    c. gives a separate term for each kind of cousin.
    d. is the least precise of all the kinship systems.
    e. indicates that all of ego's siblings have the same social status.

23. Which of the following would **not** be considered typical activities outside the house of a rural Taiwanese woman?
    a. wash clothes on the riverbank
    b. clean and pare vegetables at a communal pump
    c. mend clothes under a tree
    d. stop to rest on a bench with other women
    e. shop at the market place

24. In autumn 1981, Dutch anthropologist _____ went to Maine to check out a job at the Association of Aroostook Indians, which needed a research and development director.
    a. Lewis Henry Morgan
    b. Fred Plog
    c. G.P. Murdock
    d. Weston LaBarre
    e. Harald Prins

25. This major theoretician of nineteenth-century North American anthropology has been regarded as the founder of kinship studies.
    a. Margaret Mead
    b. Leslie White
    c. Julian Steward
    d. Lewis Henry Morgan
    e. Geoffrey Gorer

26. The production of the world's first "test-tube" baby, in a petri dish outside the womb, without sexual intercourse took place in what year?
    a. 1978
    b. 1965
    c. 1954
    d. 1988
    e. 1995

27. All societies have found some form of family and/or household organization a convenient way to deal with problems all human groups encounter. Which of the following would be problems all human groups face?
    a. how to facilitate economic cooperation between the sexes
    b. when to retire
    c. how to regulate sexual activity
    d. how to provide a proper setting for child rearing
    e. all but *b*

28. Important though family membership was for each individual in the traditional Chinese patrilineal society, it was the _____ that was regarded as the primary social unit.
    a. nuclear family
    b. extended family
    c. *tsu*
    d. *mu shoo*
    e. *chow su bao*

29. Two or more clans together constitute larger units called _____.
    a. moieties.
    b. phratries.
    c. extended families.
    d. blended families.
    e. ambilocal clans.

30. The descent system that allows each individual the option of affiliating with either the mother's or the father's descent group is known as _____ descent.
    a. double
    b. matrilineal
    c. patrilineal
    d. avunculocal
    e. ambilineal

31. In the years prior to World War II younger-generation descendants of east European Jewish immigrants sought to separate themselves from older generations while still maintaining the traditional Jewish ethic of family solidarity formed what has come to be known as _____.
    a. family circles.
    b. private clubs.
    c. cousin clubs.
    d. gangs.
    e. fraternities.

32. The _____, like Microsoft and Intel, is a corporate group.
    a. lineage
    b. clan
    c. clique
    d. cousin club
    e. fraternity

Answers to multiple-choice practice questions

1. e	9. e	17. a	25. d
2. a	10. e	18. d	26. a
3. b	11. e	19. c	27. e
4. e	12. a	20. e	28. c
5. d	13. e	21. e	29. b
6. e	14. e	22. c	30. e
7. a	15. c	23. e	31. c
8. e	16. c	24. e	32. a

True/False Practice Questions

1. _____ Cross-cousins are ideal marriage partners in an arrangement whereby lineages engage in reciprocal marriage exchanges to establish alliances.

2. _____ Omaha kinship terminology is the matrilineal equivalent of the Crow system.

3. _____ The system with the greatest number of kin terms is the Sudanese or Descriptive system.

4. _____ The kindred is a kin group that is organized laterally rather than lineally.

5. _____ The boundaries of a kindred are permanent and definite.

6. _____ Women in rural Taiwan live their lives in the walled courtyards of their husbands' households.

7. _____ It is in their relations in the outside world that women develop sufficient backing to maintain some independence under their powerful mothers-in-law.

8. _____ The shy young Taiwanese girl who enters the village as a bride is examined as frankly and suspiciously by the women as an animal that is up for sale.

9. _____ A Taiwanese girl who gossips freely about the affairs of her husband's household may find herself always on the outside of the group, or worse yet, accused of snobbery.

10. _____ In rural Taiwan women can serve as a powerful protective force for their defenseless younger members, in this way they are a very liberated force in the village.

11. _____ Even older rural Taiwanese women who have raised their sons properly retain little influence over their sons' actions, especially in activities exclusive to men.

12. _____ A Taiwanese woman is subject to an important set of rules, and to be successful she must strictly obey those rules.

13. _____ A truly successful Taiwanese woman is a rugged individualist who has learned to depend largely on herself while appearing to lean on the males in her family.

14. _____ Unilineal descent provides an easy way of restricting descent group membership so as to minimize problems of divided loyalty and the like.

15. _____ Bilateral kinship and bilateral descent cannot be used interchangeably since they different meanings.

16. _____ Descent groups don't need to clearly define membership to operate efficiently.

17. _____ In a society where descent is traced patrilineally, maternal relatives are less important.

18. _____ Double descent, whereby descent is reckoned both patrilineally and matrilineally at the same time, is very rare.

19. _____ Because of its bilateral structure, a kindred is never the same for any two persons except siblings. Thus, no two people (except siblings) belong to the same kindred.

Answers to true/false practice questions

1. T	6. F	11. F	16. F
2. F	7. T	12. F	17. F
3. T	8. T	13. T	18. T
4. T	9. T	14. T	19. T
5. F	10. F	15. T	

Practice Essays

1. Compare and contrast the social organization of the Hopi and the Chinese.

2. Many North American feminists are interested in the concept of matriarchy, sometimes confusing it with or linking it to the matrilineal descent system. Does matrilineality imply matriarchy? Use concrete examples to explore this.

3. Describe a typical woman's life in rural Taiwan from the time she enters her husband's family as a new bride to the time she reaches seniority in his household as a mother-in-law.

4. Describe how women in patrilineal societies like Taiwan actively manipulate the system to their own advantage as best they can.

5. Identify at least ten different terms that are needed to cover the concepts of "mother" and "father' in Western societies.

6. Discuss the inevitable changes that will have to occur with traditional notions of kinship and gender, due to the advent of new reproductive technologies that separate conception from birth and eggs from wombs.

7. Descent groups are convenient devices for solving a number of problems human societies commonly confront. Identify the problems and describe how a descent group solves them.

8. Discuss the forms and functions of descent groups.

9. The culture's descent system is closely tied to a society's economic base. Explain why this is so.

Chapter 11
Grouping by Sex, Age, Common Interest, and Class

Synopsis

Chapter 11 examines major kinds of nonkin organizations. Groups defined by gender, age, and common interest are described. Finally, stratified forms of social organization such as those involving class or caste are presented.

What You Should Learn from This Chapter

1. Understand the functions of nonkin groupings:
   - sex
   - age
   - common interests

2. Know how societies are stratified and the reasons for social divisions.

3. Understand the differences between class and caste-type stratification.

Key Terms

age grade

age set

apartheid

caste

common-interest association

cousins club

egalitarian society

mobility

open-class societies

social class

stratified society

symbolic indicators

verbal evaluation

Review Questions

1. Describe the separate but equal organization of the Iroquois.

2. In what ways is age grouping evidenced in North America?

3. How does one become a member of an age grade?

4. Distinguish between an age group and an age set.

5. Describe the Tiriki age-set system.

6. How and why are common-interest associations formed?

7. Historically, why have women's groups been less common than men's?

8. What functions do women's associations have?

9. What purposes do urban-oriented associations serve?

10. Describe the interstrata relationship in a stratified society.

11. Contrast an egalitarian society with a stratified society.

12. In what ways might a society be stratified?

13. Briefly describe India's caste system.

14. Compare India's caste system to the South African system of apartheid.

15. How might a stratified society beget an outcast group?

16. What are three aspects of a social-class structure?

17. Distinguish between the three ways social class are manifest in society.

18. What is social-impact assessment?

19. What role does religion play in India's caste system?

20. How and why did the Maya develop a stratified society?

21. What are "virtual" common-interest associations?

Fill-in-the-Blank

1. An age _____ is a category based on age, a stage through which people pass (such as a "teenager").

2. An age _____ is a group of people who move through life stages together (such as "baby boomers").

3. Among the _____ of South America, men and women work, eat, and sleep separately.

4. Common-interest associations used to be called _____ associations.

5. The text suggests that the caste system is present not only in India but also in _____ and _____.

6. A _____ society is one in which members do not share equally in prestige and basic resources.

7. _____ is a special form of social class in which membership is determined by birth and remains fixed for life.

8. In a class society, people are theoretically able to change their class positions through social _____.

Exercise

Briefly identify and locate the following cultures.

1. Iroquois

3. Tiriki

2. South African

4. Maya

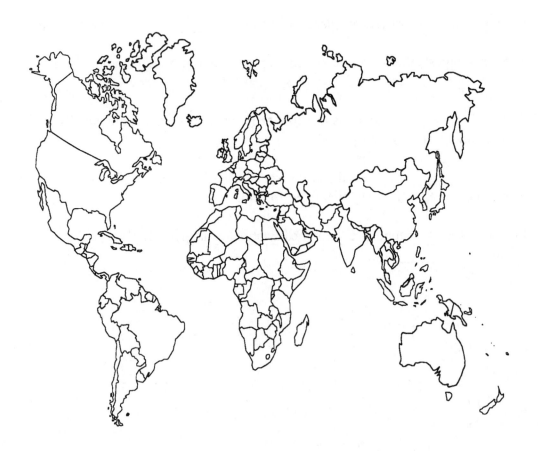

Multiple-Choice Practice Questions

1. High rates of rape appear to be associated with societies in which the roles of males and females are highly segregated, and in which there are efforts by males to be dominant over women. If this is true, we would expect the highest rate of rape to occur among the _____.
   a. Ju/'hoansi.
   b. Mundurucu.
   c. Iroquois.
   d. Mbuti.
   e. Hopi.

2. Ambilineal descent groups were a response among Jewish immigrants to urban life in North America. These groups did not recruit on the basis of age. By the late 1930s, their descendants had become so assimilated that they formed new descent groups, called _____, which excluded their parents and grandparents from membership as well as their own children until they reached legal majority or married.
   a. family circles
   b. cousins clubs
   c. age grades
   d. age sets
   e. common-interest associations

3. In literate societies that rely on the written word for accumulated wisdom, elders are often _____.
   a. treated with great respect because of their wisdom.
   b. considered to be as valuable as their weight in gold.
   c. treated like "living libraries" that contain much needed knowledge.
   d. not considered sources of information.
   e. killed when they turn sixty-five years old.

4. The following _____ are passed through by members of North American culture: toddler, teenager, senior citizen.
   a. age grades
   b. age sets
   c. social classes
   d. castes
   e. open classes

5. Which of the following statements about common-interest associations is **incorrect**?
   a. They were originally referred to in the anthropological literature as voluntary associations.
   b. Common-interest associations are more common in hunter-gatherer societies than in urban-industrial societies.
   c. Common-interest associations are intimately associated with world urbanization and increasing social complexity.
   d. Common-interest associations are found in many traditional societies.
   e. Sometimes one can join a common-interest association voluntarily, and sometimes membership is required by law.

6. The text suggests that women's participation in common-interest associations in traditional societies is often less than men's because _____.
   a. women are less sociable than men.
   b. women have no interests in common because they see each other as sexual competitors.
   c. women remain at home, isolated from other women.
   d. men prevent women from joining such groupings.
   e. women have so many opportunities to socialize that they have little need for common-interest associations.

7. In times of rapid social change _____.
   a. common-interest associations decline in significance.
   b. common-interest associations assume the roles and functions formerly held by kinship or age groups.
   c. women form common-interest associations whereas men retain their membership in age and kinship groups.
   d. men are able to adapt whereas women are not.
   e. the role of the elderly becomes more important as the society adjusts to change.

8. A society composed of several groups that differ in their access to resources and prestige is said to be _____.
   a. stratified.
   b. unfair.
   c. immoral.
   d. egalitarian.
   e. open.

9. A/An _____ is a special form of social class in which membership is determined by birth and remains fixed for life.
   a. clan
   b. phratry
   c. common-interest association
   d. age group
   e. caste

10. Symbolic indicators may not always be reliable in helping you assess someone's class status. Which of the following is an example of this?
    a. A common form of recreation of lower-class males is playing pool at the local beer joint.
    b. A con man from a lower-class background wears a tuxedo when he tries to sell you shares in a nonexistent corporation.
    c. According to Emily Post, one can always identify upper-crust families by the presence of a day maid.
    d. Demille O'Hara, striving to return to the simplicity of life as lived by his tribal ancestors, lets his day maid go.
    e. *b* and *d*

11. The ability to change one's class position is known as _____.
    a. open class.
    b. egalitarian.
    c. social mobility.
    d. indicative of common-interest societies.
    e. inevitable.

12. The degree of social mobility in a stratified society is related to _____.
    a. the prevailing kind of family organization.
    b. its ideology.
    c. the number of different common-interest associations it has.
    d. the difference between its richest and poorest classes.
    e. genetic factors.

13. Which of the following could have contributed to the emergence of social stratification?
    a. All human beings want to be looked up to by their fellow members of society.
    b. Certain descent groups may have monopolized activities that turned out to play an important role in their society (such as propitiation of the gods in a horticultural society exposed to unpredictable weather).
    c. An ethnic group with an economic or military advantage (such as knowledge of intensive agriculture or possession of firearms) that enters a foreign territory may become the ruling class within that area.
    d. all of the above
    e. none of the above

14. Among the first groups to be targeted in the genocide that occurred in Rwanda were _____.
    a. human rights activists.
    b. university professors.
    c. opposition parties.
    d. journalists.
    e. *a, c,* and *d*

15. As the killing spread to the rural areas of Rwanda, it became a program of genocide specifically targeted at the _____.
    a. Hutu.
    b. Tutsi.
    c. Twa.
    d. !Kung San.
    e. Kikuyu.

16. According to the Original Study "Genocide in Rwanda," a _____ requires motive, means, and opportunity.
    a. wrong
    b. crime
    c. transgression
    d. atrocity
    e. violation

17. Which of the following are the three main groups in Rwandan society?
    a. the Nuer, Azande, and Mende
    b. the Kapauku, Kaluli, and the Karumba
    c. Twa, Hutu, and Tutsi
    d. Yoruba, Swazi, and Tsembaga
    e. Shuar, Yanomami, and Toda

18. Rwanda was once ruled by what European country?
    a. France
    b. Germany
    c. England
    d. Belgium
    e. Holland

19. The best way to identify an individual as a Twa, Hutu, or Tutsi; is _____.
    a. knowledge of the person's ancestry.
    b. possession of an identity card.
    c. height.
    d. language.
    e. *a* and *b*

20. A kind of policy research frequently done by an anthropologists is called a
    _____.
    a. ethnology.
    b. ethnography.
    c. participant observation.
    d. social impact assessment.
    e. need assessment.

21. In the U.S., any project requiring a federal permit or licence, or using federal funds,
    by law must be preceded by a _____.
    a. need assessment.
    b. archaeological assessment.
    c. cultural impact assessment.
    d. assessment of feasibility.
    e. social impact statement.

22. Anthropologist _____ was hired to carry out a social impact assessment
    of a water diversion project in New Mexico.
    a. Sue Ellen Jacobs
    b. Harald Prins
    c. R.M. Bradfield
    d. P.R. Sanday
    e. Fred Plog

23. What the term _____ really refers to are those associations not based on sex, age, kinship, marriage, or territory that result from an act of joining.
    a. clan
    b. age grade
    c. voluntary association
    d. neighborhood association
    e. womens' auxiliary

24. Which of the following is **not** an example of a common-interest organization?
    a. the American Federation of Labor
    b. the National Rifle Association
    c. the Navajo Nation
    d. the Aryan Nation
    e. the Green Party

25. Which of the following would be reasons for the decline in membership in common-interest associations in the United States?
    a. viewing television
    b. frequent moves
    c. long working hours
    d. the Internet
    e. all of the above

26. Social scientists have observed that today, with outright unemployment at historically low levels, the _____ provide/s a pool of cheap labor.
    a. lower castes
    b. middle-class
    c. underclass
    d. mentally-challenged
    e. pariah groups

27. In which of the following societies are men and women rigidly segregated in what they do?
    a. Seneca
    b. Oneida
    c. Mohawk
    d. Onondaga
    e. all of the above

28. Age grouping is so familiar and so important that it and _____
    sometimes have been called the only universal factors for determining a persons's
    position in society.
    a. height
    b. weight
    c. eye color
    d. sex
    e. shoe size

29. The members of a/an _____ usually remain closely associated
    throughout their lives, or at least most of their lives.
    a. fraternity
    b. sorority
    c. union
    d. kindred
    e. age set

30. All stratified societies offer at least some _____, and this helps to ease
    the strains in any system of inequality.
    a. stability
    b. reliability
    c. instability
    d. mobility
    e. shakiness

31. In which of the following ways are societies stratified?
    a. gender
    b. age
    c. social class
    d. caste
    e. all of the above

Answers to multiple-choice practice questions

1. b	9. e	17. c	25. e
2. b	10. e	18. d	26. c
3. d	11. c	19. e	27. e
4. a	12. a	20. d	28. d
5. b	13. d	21. e	29. e
6. e	14. e	22. a	30. d
7. b	15. b	23. c	31. e
8. a	16. b	24. c	

True/False Practice Questions

1. _____ Division of labor by sex is characteristic of all human societies.

2. _____ Usually an increase in the number of common-interest associations is associated with urbanization, but these associations are also found in traditional societies.

3. _____ Castes are strongly exogamous.

4. _____ Mobility refers to the ability to change one's class position.

5. _____ An age grade is a group of people initiated into the group at the same time who move though the series of categories together.

6. _____ According to the original study in your textbook "Genocide in Rwanda," Rwanda has long been known as a true nation in Africa.

7. _____ The three groups in Rwanda the Twa, Hutu, and Tutsi are actually three different strata of the same group.

8. _____ It is easy to tell which group a Rwandan belongs to by his/her height.

9. _____ The major factors in the violence in Rwanda is the fact that the groups involved speak a different language, and have a different culture and religion.

10. _____ Other contributing factors to the violence in Rwanda is that the groups involved live in different places and have a strong sense of tribal pride.

11. _____ The crime of genocide in Rwanda was mis-diagnosed by the international community as spontaneous ethnic violence.

12. _____ One of the major objections to the construction of the water diversion project in New Mexico is that it would result in the obliteration of the three-hundred-year-old irrigation system structures.

13. _____ Observers have noted a recent decrease in participation in all sorts of common-interest associations.

14. _____ According to Mundurucu beliefs men have always ruled over women.

15. _____ Like age grades, age sets cease to exist after a specified number of years.

16. _____ Common-interest associations have proliferated modern society, but are not found in many traditional societies.

17. _____ The Indian caste system has absolutely no flexibility and/or mobility.

Answers to true/false practice questions

1. T	6. T	11. T	16. F
2. T	7. T	12. T	17. F
3. F	8. F	13. T	
4. T	9. F	14. F	
5. F	10. F	15. F	

Practice Matching

Match the culture with its characteristic.

1. _____Iroquois

2. _____Tiriki

3. _____New York Jews

4. _____South Africans

5. _____Maya

a. Cousins clubs in urban immigrant society.

b. African nomadic pastoralists with an age set/age grade system.

c. Castelike social organization based on racial divisions.

d. Native Americans with separate but equal gender organization.

e. Stratified society of pre-Columbian Central America.

Answers to practice matching

1. d   2. b   3. a   4. c   5. e

Practice Essays

1. Marx felt that religion was "the opiate of the masses," claiming that it was often used by the upper classes to perpetuate their own dominance. Can this perspective be applied to the Indian caste system? Would it be ethnocentric to do so?

2. Describe age grouping in Western society, using as an example the cousins clubs of North America.

3. Because of the nature of Rwandan society, the genocide in Rwanda required a mass mobilization of killers. What is the nature of society in Rwanda? Explain.

4. What were the findings of the social impact assessment of the water diversion project in New Mexico?

5. Although important differences exist, there are nonetheless interesting similarities between Mundurucu beliefs and those of traditional European culture. Discuss those similarities.

6. Compare and contrast stratified societies with egalitarian societies.

7. Some observers have noted a recent decline in participation in all types of common-interest organizations, at least in North America. What is the explanation for this decline? Explain.

Chapter 12
Political Organization and
Maintenance of Order

Synopsis

Chapter 12 defines politics as a system that maintains social order within and between societies. Decentralized and centralized type of political systems are described and an attempt is made to define "law" in cross-cultural terms. The concepts of authority and legitimacy are discussed and various kinds of leadership are examined.

What You Should Learn from This Chapter

1. Know the four major kinds of political organization:
   • bands
   • tribes
   • chiefdoms
   • states

2. Understand how internal political and social control is maintained in different political systems.

3. Understand how external affairs are conducted in different political systems.

4. Understand how conflicts are resolved and the functions of law.

5. Recognize the impact of religion on social control.

Key Terms

adjudication

band

centralized system

chiefdom

law

mediation

nation

negotiation

political organization

sanctions

segmentary lineage system

state

tribe

uncentralized system

world view

Review Questions

1. What are the four basic kinds of political systems?

2. What kinds of societies typically have uncentralized systems?

3. How is authority conferred in a band?

4. How is authority conferred in a tribe?

5. Distinguish between the segmentary lineage system and the clan.

6. What is the role of the leopard-skin chief of the Nuer?

7. What is the function of age-grade systems in the political structure of tribes?

8. Describe the role of the *tonowi* among the Kapauku Papuans.

9. What kinds of societies typically have centralized political systems?

10. Distinguish between nation and state.

11. What has women's role generally been in political leadership?

12. Describe women's role in Igbo society.

13. How is social control generally maintained in bands and tribes?

14. How do internalized controls guide behavior?

15. Distinguish between positive and negative sanctions.

16. Distinguish between informal and formal sanctions.

17. What are the limits on power in Bedouin society?

18. Why is the definition of law destined to be inexact?

19. What are the functions of law?

20. Differentiate between negotiation, adjudication, and mediation.

21. How are disputes handled by the Kpelle?

22. Why might warfare be so prominent in food-producing societies?

23. Compare the world view of the Abenaki with that of the Iroquois.

24. Distinguish between force and legitimacy.

25. In what ways is religion connected with politics?

26. What does the term *political organization* refer to?

27. Identify three groups of people, and the area where they live, who do not practice warfare as we know it.

Fill-in-the-Blank

1. The term _____ refers to the system of social relationships that is connected with the maintenance of public order.

2. The term _____ refers to an administrative system having specialized personnel.

3. Anthropologists have identified four types of political systems; two are said to be _____ and two _____.

4. An egalitarian, autonomous small group composed of related people who occupy a single region is called a _____.

5. All humans were food foragers living in band-type organizations until about _____ years ago.

6. The _____ are an example of a society practicing band-level organization.

7. Most conflict in bands is settled by informal means, and decisions are usually made by _____.

8. A _____ is a larger grouping than a band and is linked to a specific territory.

9. A form of political organization in which a larger group is broken up into clans that are then divided into lineages, is called a _____ lineage system.

10. Among the Nuer, the tendency for widespread feuding to occur among lineages is counterbalanced by the actions of the _____.

11. In tribal societies of Melanesia, a type of leader called the _____ or *tonowi* is prevalent.

12. A _____ is a ranked society in which every member has a position in the hierarchy.

13. Chiefdoms are linked to _____ economic systems.

14. The Swazi have a _____-level political system.

15. States are typically linked to _____ subsistence patterns.

16. An example of a society in which women play a notably strong political role is the _____.

17. The Wape of New Guinea use belief in_____as a means of social control.

18. In North America we rely on both external and _____ controls to maintain social order.

19. Among the Bedouin _____ sanctions restrict the inappropriate use of power by those in authority.

20. The Inuit use _____ as a means of resolving conflict.

21. Malinowski distinguished law from _____ by whether there was a "definite social machinery of binding force."

22. Western societies make a distinction between _____ law, involving offenses committed against individuals, and _____ law, involving offenses committed against the state.

23. Disputes may be settled by _____, the use of direct argument and compromise by the disputing parties, or by _____, settlement through the assistance of an unbiased third party.

24. Warfare is most closely linked to the _____-type political system.

Exercises

I. Fill in the chart below, giving examples of each of the major types of political systems and describing their general characteristics. You can use this to study from later.

TYPES OF POLITICAL SYSTEMS

Type	Example	Characteristics
Band		
Tribe		
Chiefdom		
State		

II. Briefly identify and locate the following cultures.

1. Nuer

4. Bedouin

2. Kpelle

5. Abenaki

3. Igbo

6. Swazi

Multiple-Choice Practice Questions

1. The term "government" may be defined as _____.
   a. a kinship-based age set.
   b. those aspects of social organization concerned with coordination and regulation of public behavior.
   c. the informal leadership of a Ju/'hoansi hunter-gatherer band.
   d. common-interest association focusing on political events.
   e. an administrative system having specialized personnel.

2. Bands and tribes are both _____.
   a. centralized.
   b. associated with industrialism.
   c. dependent on age groups for political organization.
   d. uncentralized and egalitarian.
   e. hierarchical in social organization.

3. The form of social organization typical of hunter-gatherers is the _____, whereas horticulture and pastoralism are usually associated with the form of social organization called the _____.
   a. tribe/chiefdom
   b. tribe/state
   c. tribe/band
   d. band/chiefdom
   e. band/tribe

4. The "leopard-skin chief" among the Nuer _____.
   a. is the head of the largest and most powerful clan.
   b. is the head of the dominant matrilineage.
   c. has the authority to force feuding lineages to accept "blood cattle" and stop feuding.
   d. tries to mediate between feuding sides but does not have political power.
   e. is the totem of one of the Nuer lineages.

5. Age-grade systems and common-interest associations are effective methods of integrating small autonomous units such as bands into larger social units. These methods may be described as _____ systems of political organization.
   a. segmentary
   b. negotiated
   c. state
   d. nonkinship
   e. kinship

6. A _____ is a ranked society in which every member has a position in the hierarchy, and an individual's status is determined by membership in a descent group.
   a. band
   b. tribe
   c. chiefdom
   d. state
   e. kindred

7. The state is distinctive in the extensiveness of its legitimate use of _____ to regulate the affairs of its citizens.
   a. kinship
   b. force
   c. chiefs
   d. religion
   e. gossip

8. In a chiefdom, an individual's status is determined by membership in a _____.
   a. government.
   b. social class.
   c. bureaucracy.
   d. descent group.
   e. secret society.

9. A cross-cultural comparison of systems of political organization reveals that _____.
   a. many women who hold high office do so by virtue of their relationship to men.
   b. many women in positions of leadership adopt characteristics of temperament that are usually considered masculine.
   c. in a number of societies, women have as much political power as men.
   d. women may play an important role in political decisions even when they are not visible public leaders.
   e. all of the above

10. At he heart of political organization is _____.
    a. control of unacceptable social behavior.
    b. the legitimate use of force to maintain order.
    c. unequal access to power.
    d. the dominance of males over females.
    e. the development of egalitarian relationships.

11. Sanctions refer to _____.
    a. internalized social controls.
    b. holy behavior.
    c. externalized social controls.
    d. decadent behavior.
    e. ritualized behavior.

12. _____ sanctions attempt to precisely and explicitly regulate people's behavior. They can be positive (such as military decorations) or negative (such as imprisonment).
    a. Hierarchical
    b. Egalitarian
    c. Informal
    d. Formal
    e. Magical

13. In centralized societies, antisocial behavior is usually dealt with in a court system by the use of formal, negative sanctions involving the application of abstract rules and the use of force. The primary aim is _____.
    a. to help the victim.
    b. to renew social relations between the victim and the perpetrator of the crime.
    c. to prevent witchcraft from being used.
    d. to assign and punish guilt.
    e. to provide a good show for the spectators.

14. The functions of law include _____.
    a. the definition of proper behavior in particular circumstances so that everyone is clear about their rights and duties.
    b. protecting the wealthy from the poor.
    c. redefining what is proper behavior when situations change.
    d. allocating authority to use coercion to enforce sanctions
    e. all but *b*

15. A method of resolving disputes in which the disputing parties voluntarily arrive at a mutually satisfactory agreement is called _____.
    a. negotiation.
    b. mediation.
    c. adjudication.
    d. use of sanctions.
    e. law.

16. Which of the following are likely to be associated with warfare?
    a. centralized political systems
    b. the rise of cities
    c. a technology that supports population growth
    d. possession of complex, valuable property
    e. all of the above

17. An exploitative world view is more likely to exist in which of the following technologies?
    a. food foraging
    b. horticulture
    c. pastoralism
    d. intensive agriculture
    e. all of the above except *a*

18. Power based on force does not usually last very long; to be effective, it must be considered _____.
    a. legitimate.
    b. mediated.
    c. negotiated.
    d. subject to sanctions.
    e. inevitable.

19. _____, which seem to be associated with the weak and with dependents, provides one of several checks on the abuse of authority in Bedouin society.
    a. Ostracism
    b. Informal sanctions
    c. Legal sanctions
    d. Paralegal sanctions
    e. Supernatural sanctions

20. Another agent of control in societies, whether or not they possess centralized political systems, may be _____.
    a. witchcraft.
    b. sorcerers.
    c. ostracism.
    d. fines set by judges.
    e. warriors.

21. An important pioneer in the anthropological study of law was _____.
    a. A.L. Kroeber.
    b. George Peter Murdock.
    c. John Wesley Powell.
    d. E. Adamson Hoebel.
    e. Peggy Reeves Sanday.

22. The field of _____ is one of growing anthropological involvement and employment.
    a. ethnoscience
    b. ethnology
    c. dispute control
    d. dispute management
    e. assertiveness training

23. In 1980, _____ as a practitioner of dispute management, helped the U.S. and the Soviet Union replace their obsolete "hot line" with fully equipped nuclear crisis centers in each capital.
    a. Sue Ellen Jacobs
    b. William L. Ury
    c. Laura Nader
    d. L. Abu-Lughod
    e. Harald Prins

24. When one refers to the way power is distributed and embedded in society, one is referring to a society's _____.
    a. social organization.
    b. military structure.
    c. political ideology.
    d. class structure.
    e. political organization.

25. The ability to control others' behavior, whether organizing a seal hunt or raising a military force, has to do with the way power is distributed and embedded in a society, or its _____.
    a. political organization.
    b. social class structure.
    c. political ideology.
    d. police force.
    e. social system.

26. To support the view that humans are innately warlike observers cite the behavior of people such as the _____, who are portrayed as living in a constant state of war.
    a. Apache
    b. Comanche
    c. Ju/'hoansi
    d. Mende
    e. Yanomami

27. It is clear that war is not a universal phenomenon, for in various parts of the world there are societies that do not practice warfare as we know it. Which of the following groups of people is **not** an example of a group that does not practice warfare?
    a. the Bushman of southern Africa
    b. the Arapesh of New Guinea
    c. the Hopi of the American southwest
    d. the Yanomami of South America
    e. all of the above are warlike

28. Scholars have identified four basic kinds of political systems and categorized them into uncentralized and centralized. Which of the following would be considered uncentralized systems?
    a. chiefdoms
    b. tribes
    c. states
    d. bands
    e. *b* and *d*

29. The _____ do not think of government as something fixed and all-powerful, and to them leadership was not vested in a central authority.
    a. Navajo
    b. Melanesians
    c. Mayan
    d. Yanomami
    e. Gururumba

30. In his classic study of segmentary lineage organizations, Marshall Sahlins described how this system works among the _____.
    a. Kapauku.
    b. Nuer.
    c. Tiriki.
    d. Ju/'hoansi.
    e. Onondaga.

31. _____ systems provide a tribal society with a means of political integration beyond the kin group.
    a. Age-grade
    b. Common-interest association
    c. Segmentary lineage
    d. Kindred
    e. Clan

32. An important pioneer in the anthropological study of law was _____.
    a. E.E. Evans-Pritchard.
    b. Marshal Sahlins.
    c. Leo Pospisil.
    d. E. Adamson Hoebel.
    e. A.R. Radcliffe-Brown.

Answers to multiple-choice practice questions

1. e	9. e	17. e	25. a
2. d	10. a	18. a	26. e
3. e	11. c	19. e	27. d
4. d	12. d	20. a	28. e
5. d	13. d	21. d	29. a
6. c	14. e	22. d	30. b
7. b	15. a	23. b	31. a
8. d	16. e	24. e	32. d

True/False Practice Questions

1. _____ In the French monarchy under Louis XIV, the king was the state in an important sense.

2. _____ Until recently many non-Western peoples had no fixed form of government in the sense that Westerners understand the term.

3. _____ The Ju/'hoansi have a tribal-type political organization.

4. _____ The Big Man of the Kapauku is called tonowi.

5. _____ A classic example of a segmentary lineage system is found among the Nuer.

6. _____ In Bedouin society, because those in authority are expected to treat their dependents with some respect, they must draw as little attention as possible to the inequality of their relationship.

7. _____   The use of fictive kin terms serves to mask relations of inequality in Bedouin society.

8. _____   Among the Bedouins, the tyranny of those in power is accepted as natural and tolerated.

9. _____   A Bedouin woman can resist a tyrannical husband by leaving for her natal home "angry." This is the approved response to abuse in Bedouin society.

10. _____   Bedouin women have less recourse against tyrannical fathers or guardians, but various informal means to resist the imposition of unwanted decisions do exist. Although, suicide is not one of them.

11. _____   Figures of authority in Bedouin society are vulnerable to their dependents because their positions rest on the respect these people are willing to give them.

12. _____   What anthropologists involved with dispute management are trying to do is to help create a culture of negotiation in a world where adversarial, win-lose attitudes are out of step with the increasingly interdependent relations between people.

13. _____   The term political organization refers to the way power is distributed and embedded in society.

14. _____   It is clear that war is a universal phenomena.

15. _____   Among food foragers, with their uncentralized political systems, warfare is all but unknown.

16. _____   Among the Igbo of Midwestern Nigeria, women were not allowed positions in the administrative hierarchy.

17. _____   Western societies do not clearly distinguish offenses against the state, called crimes, from offenses against individuals, called torts.

18. _____   Every society develops customs designed to encourage conformity to social norms.

Answers to true/false practice questions

1. T	6. T	11. T	16. F
2. T	7. T	12. T	17. F
3. F	8. F	13. T	18. T
4. T	9. T	14. F	
5. T	10. F	15. T	

Practice Matching

Match the culture with its characteristic.

1. _____Nuer

2. _____Swazi

3. _____Igbo
4. _____Wape

5. _____Abenaki

a. Nigerian society in which men and women occupy separate political spheres.
b. Northeastern Native American foragers in the historic past that lived in harmony with their environment.
c. A southeast African nation.
d. A New Guinea people in the historical past with effective informal and internalized controls.
e. East African herders with a segmentary lineage system.

Answers to practice matching

1. e   2. c   3. a   4. d   5. b

Practice Essays

1. Why has the state-type system expanded to encompass most of the globe today? Explore how band, tribe, and chiefdom organizations might persist within a world order based primarily on states.

2. Identify and discuss the limits on the power of authority figures in Bedouin society. That is, what options are open to dependents in Bedouin society that would allow them to check an oppressive authority figure.

3. Who is William L. Ury? What is his area of expertise? What is he trying to accomplish?

4. Describe how the segmentary lineage system works among the Nuer.

5. Why do wars occur? Is the need to wage war an instinctive feature of the human personality? Explain.

Chapter 13
Religion and the Supernatural

Synopsis

In Chapter 13 the text discusses the universality of religion, considering the functions served by religious belief and ritual in the social order. Various kinds of supernatural beings are compared and the relationships among magic, science, and religion are examined. The role of religion in culture change is also discussed.

What You Should Learn from This Chapter

1. Understand why religion exists.

2. Understand the various forms of religious belief:
   • animatism
   • animism
   • shamanism
   • belief in ancestral spirits
   • belief in gods and goddesses

3. Understand the relationship between religion, magic, and witchcraft and the functions of each.

4. Understand the role of religion in cultural change.

Key Terms and Names

animatism

animism

contagious magic

divination

Edward B. Tylor

imitative magic

incorporation

pantheon

priest or priestess

religion

revitalization movements

rites of intensification

rites of passage

separation

shaman

transition

witchcraft

Review Questions

1. What is the relationship between science and religion?

2. Why might there be less religion, as defined in your textbook, in more complex societies?

3. What are three categories of supernatural beings?

4. What is the role of gods and goddesses in many societies?

5. How does healing occur among the Ju/'hoansi?

6. What purpose do ancestral spirits serve?

7. In what type of society is one likely to find animism?

8. Distinguish between animism and animatism.

9. How does mana perpetuate itself?

10. In what type of society is one likely to find priestesses?

11. How are shamans made and how do they carry out their work?

12. What benefits do people derive from enlisting the services of a shaman?

13. What are two main types of ritual?

14. What are the three stages in a rite of passage, according to Van Gennep?

15. Why are rites of intensification performed?

16. Distinguish between the two fundamental principles of magic.

17. In what ways does the Tewa origin myth reflect Tewa social structure?

18. How are witch hunts used for societal control?

19. What is the role of witchcraft among the Navajo?

20. What are the psychological functions of religion?

21. What are the social functions of religion?

22. How and why do revitalization movements emerge?

Fill-in-the-Blank

1. Alfonso Ortiz was an anthropologist of _____ ancestry who studied the religious beliefs of the Tewa.

2. In Tewa society the _____ mediate between the human and spiritual worlds and between the two moieties.

3. In the nineteenth century European thinkers believed that _____ would eventually eclipse religion.

4. The set of gods and goddesses in a society are called its _____.

5. In most societies with subsistence bases in _____ or _____, deities are conceptualized as masculine.

6. A belief that nature is animated by spirits is called _____.

7. A concept of impersonal power, such as mana, is called _____.

8. _____ are specialists who have acquired spiritual power, which they can use on behalf of human clients.

9. _____ was a pioneer in the study of rites of passage.

10. When Mende girls are initiated into adult society, they undergo _____.

11. A ceremony to bring rain to a drought-stricken community is a _____.

12. The three stages of a life crisis ritual are _____, _____, and _____.

13. _____ wrote *The Golden Bough*.

14. _____ magic is based on the assumption that things that are similar to each other have an effect on each other.

15. Assuming that a person's fingernail clippings, hair, blood, and so on retain a spiritual connection to that person is the basis for _____ magic.

16. Among the Navajo, _____ is a way of expression and channeling hostile feelings.

17. A _____ is a social movement whose intent is to totally transform a society.

18. Anthropologist _____ studied the stages typical of revitalization movements.

Exercise

Briefly identify and locate the following cultures discussed in the chapter.

1. Tewa

3. Ibibio

2. Sioux

4. Mende

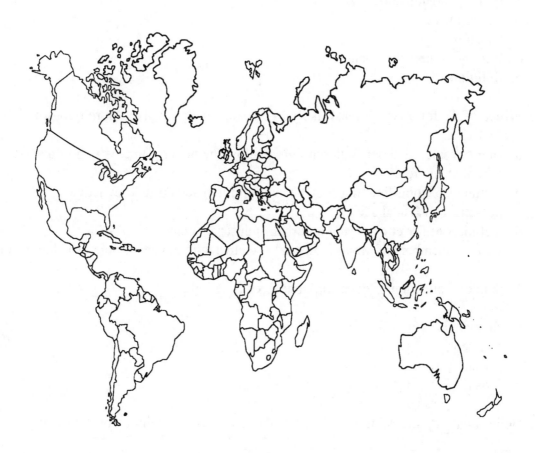

Multiple-Choice Practice Questions

1. Islamic fundamentalism in Iran and Christian fundamentalism in the United States demonstrate that _____.
   a. science has succeeded in destroying religion in the twentieth century.
   b. religious activity is prominent in the lives of social elites.
   c. science meets basic needs.
   d. religion is a powerful and dynamic force in society today.
   e. science is wrong.

2. _____ may be defined as the beliefs and patterns of behavior by which people try to control those aspects of the universe that are otherwise beyond their control.
   a. Political organization
   b. Government
   c. Kinship
   d. Common-interest associations
   e. Religion

3. Which of the following is **least** likely to be extensively involved in religious beliefs and activities?
   a. single women with ten children living below the poverty line, who dropped out of school at age fourteen
   b. members of food-foraging societies with limited scientific knowledge
   c. peasants in a feudal society
   d. members of lower classes in an urban-industrial society
   e. wealthy members of urban-industrial societies with advanced scientific knowledge

4. A people's collection of gods and goddesses is called a _____.
   a. mana.
   b. shaman.
   c. pantheon.
   d. priest.
   e. fetish.

5. Belief in a supreme being who controls the universe is usually associated with _____.
   a. bands.
   b. tribes.
   c. chiefdoms.
   d. states.
   e. multinational corporations.

6. If religious belief reflects the structure of society, in which types of society would you expect to find widespread belief in ancestral spirits?
   a. those in which descent groups play a major role in social organization
   b. those with a disproportionately large number of old people
   c. those with a disproportionately large number of young people
   d. those in which neolocal marital residence is the rule
   e. those with egocentric systems such as the kindred

7. The belief that nature is animated with spirits is called _____.
   a. animation.
   b. anima.
   c. animatism.
   d. animism.
   e. ennui.

8. A _____ is a full-time religious specialist who occupies an office that has a certain rank and function.
   a. shaman
   b. priest
   c. witch
   d. magician
   e. diviner

9. In acting as a healer, the shaman _____.
   a. accurately diagnoses medical problems.
   b. may improve the patient's state of mind, which aids in recovery.
   c. may be coping with his or her own problems by becoming intensely involved with the problems of others.
   d. provides reassurance to the community through an elaborate drama that may involve trickery.
   e. all but *a*

10. Ceremonies such as bar mitzvah, elaborate wedding ceremonies, baby showers, and graduation parties that help individuals make major changes in their lives are referred to as rites of _____.
    a. transition.
    b. intensification.
    c. separation.
    d. passage.
    e. incorporation.

11. A funeral ceremony may be regarded as _____.
    a. a rite of passage.
    b. an opportunity to restore the equilibrium of the group.
    c. an opportunity for individuals to express their feelings in a structured way that ensures continuation of society.
    d. a rite of intensification.
    e. all of the above

12. In *The Golden Bough,* _____ distinguished between religion and magic.
    a. Bronislaw Malinowski
    b. Franz Boas
    c. Sir James Frazer
    d. Sir Edward Tylor
    e. Clifford Geertz

13. Many magical incantations require the use of fingernail clippings of the intended victim. This is an example of _____.
    a. imitative magic.
    b. contagious magic.
    c. witch magic.
    d. nightmare magic.
    e. scientific thinking.

14. Magic involves the manipulation of powers for good or evil, whereas witchcraft involves the possession of an innate power used for _____.
    a. religious purposes.
    b. scientific reasons.
    c. malevolent or benevolent purposes.
    d. traditional societies.
    e. societies that lack religion.

15. Religion, magic, and witchcraft are all **similar** in which of the following ways?
    a. They all disappear once modern education and scientific training expand.
    b. They all share the common goal of improving social relationships within a community.
    c. They are all associated with morose nonconformists who try to destroy society.
    d. They provide explanations of events and are mechanisms of social control.
    e. They are all morally neutral.

16. A belief in _____ enables people to explain why things go wrong by blaming certain individuals who are said to have the internal psychic ability to cause harm to others.
    a. witchcraft
    b. magic
    c. divination
    d. contagion
    e. evil

17. Which of the following illustrate the psychological functions of religion?
    a. Among the Holy Ghost People of the United States, handling snakes and drinking strychnine is a common feature of their worship; one explanation of this behavior is that by confronting the possibility of death, they achieve a sense of awe and transcendence.
    b. An Islamic judge who orders the hand of a thief cut off can sleep soundly at night because he thinks of himself as merely the agent of divinely inspired justice.
    c. The Tewa Indian origin myth provides every Tewa with a sense of this place in an orderly universe.
    d. A person raised in the Catholic religion feels tremendous guilt when she/he commits a wrong.
    e. all of the above

18. A _____ is a deliberate effort by members of a society to construct a more satisfying culture.
    a. divination
    b. rite of intensification
    c. fetish
    d. segmentary lineage system
    e. revitalization movement

19. Which of the following statements about revitalization movements is **incorrect**?
    a. The purpose of revitalization movements is to reform society.
    b. Revitalization movements always fail because they require too much change to be tolerated.
    c. All known major religions, including Judaism, Christianity, and Islam, began as revitalization movements.
    d. Revitalization movements may be completely unrealistic.
    e. Revitalization movements may be adaptive and give rise to long-lasting religions.

20. N/um generally remains dormant in a healer until an effort is made to activate it. Among the ways to activate n/um are _____.
    a. trance dance.
    b. hallucinogenic drugs.
    c. medicinal curing ceremony.
    d. solo singing.
    e. all but *b*

21. In southern Africa's Swaziland all types of illnesses are generally thought to be caused by _____ or _____.
    a. viruses/bacteria
    b. negative karma/negative attitude
    c. sorcery/loss of ancestral protection
    d. poor hygiene/poverty
    e. none of the above

22. Which of the following have the Swazi **not** traditionally relied upon for treatment of disease?
    a. herbalists
    b. diviner mediums
    c. Christian faith healers
    d. general practitioners
    e. they rely on all of the above

23. In a country where there is one traditional healer for every 110 people, but only one physician for every 10,000, the potential benefit of cooperation between physicians and healers seems self-evident. However, it was unrecognized until proposed by anthropologist _____.
    a. Edward C. Green.
    b. Harald Prins.
    c. Sir Edward B. Tylor.
    d. William L. Ury.
    e. R.R. Marett.

24. Religion is viewed most simply as organized belief in the _____, and all fulfill numerous social and psychological needs.
    a. Christianity
    b. social system
    c. supernatural
    d. prevailing culture
    e. magic

25. _____ is considered a "New Age" religion.
    a. Wicca
    b. Reform Judaism
    c. New Catholicism
    d. Seventh Day Adventist
    e. Whateverism

26. In addition to so-called "New Age" enthusiasts, faith healers and many other evangelists among fundamentalist Christians share most of the characteristics of _____.
    a. Buddhism.
    b. Shintoism.
    c. Taoism.
    d. shamanism.
    e. socialism.

27. The meanings ascribed to sensations experienced in altered states and made of their content are _____ determined, hence local traditions always vary in their detail.
    a. politically
    b. economically
    c. biologically
    d. culturally
    e. hallucinagenically

28. In 1996, a Gallup poll found that _____ percent of the respondents believed the it might be possible that the dead might be able to contact the living.
    a. 22
    b. 5
    c. 50
    d. 42
    e. 12

29. Anthropologist _____ defined religion as "a set of rituals, rationalized by myth, which mobilizes supernatural powers for the purpose of achieving or preventing transformations of state in man and nature."
    a. E.E. Evans-Pritchard
    b. E. Adamson Hoebel
    c. Hilda Kuper
    d. A.R. Radcliffe-Brown
    e. Anthony F.C. Wallace

30. The _____ Indians maintained that each person had a personal spirit that could detach itself and travel about apart from the body, while the latter remained inert.
    a. Cayuga
    b. Hopi
    c. Cheyenne
    d. Penobscot
    e. Mayan

31. In the United States millions of people have learned something about shamans through reading _____ accounts of his experiences with Don Juan, the Yaqui Indian shaman.
    a. R.R. Marett's
    b. Carlos Castaneda's
    c. Edward B. Tylor's
    d. Laura Nader's
    e. Colin Turnbull's

32. The rites of passage that help individuals through the crucial crisis of their lives can be divided into three stages. Which of the following would be those stages?
    a. separation
    b. transition
    c. incorporation
    d. acquisition
    e. all but *d*

33. Widely known among American Indians are the _____, who possess a detailed concept of witchcraft.
    a. Algonkian
    b. Cree
    c. Gros Ventre
    d. Navajo
    e. Shoshone

34. In the United States, _____ is an example of a revitalization movement that is enormously successful in gaining acceptance in the wider society.
    a. the Unification Church
    b. Mormonism
    c. the Branch Davidian
    d. the Heaven's Gate cult
    e. Jonestown

Answers to multiple-choice practice questions

1. d	10. d	19. b	28. a
2. e	11. e	20. e	29. e
3. e	12. c	21. c	30. d
4. c	13. b	22. d	31. b
5. d	14. c	23. a	32. e
6. a	15. d	24. c	33. d
7. d	16. a	25. a	34. b
8. b	17. e	26. d	
9. e	18. e	27. d	

True/False Practice Questions

1. _____ The belief that nature is animated by spirits is called animism.

2. _____ Rituals reinforce social solidarity and thus enable individuals and groups to get through crisis.

3. _____ Rites of intensification help individuals get through a crisis.

4. _____ Religion provides an orderly model of the universe and reduces fear and anxiety.

5. _____ Interceding with the spirits and drawing out their invisible arrows is the task of (Ju/'hoansi) healers.

6. _____ Among the Ju/'hoansi only men can possess the powerful healing force called *n/um*.

7. _____ *N/um* is the Ju/'hoansi equivalent of *mana*.

8. _____ The trances that healers go into are considered harmless; they simply lose consciousness.

9. _____ The power of healers' n/um is all that is thought to protect the healer in a trance from actual death.

10. _____ Today biomedical germ theory is universally accepted in societies around the world.

11. _____ Religion is viewed most simply as organized belief in the supernatural, that does not fulfill any social and psychological needs.

12. _____ Science, with its creation of new technologies, has helped diminish religious practice in the United States.

13. _____ Faith healers and many other evangelists among fundamentalist Christians have nothing in common with shamanism.

14. _____ The meanings ascribed to sensations experienced in altered states and made of their content are culturally determined.

15. _____ In fact, the custom of clitoridectomy is practiced by some in New York State.

16. _____ Far from causing the death of religion, the growth of scientific knowledge, by producing new anxieties and raising new questions about human existence, may have contributed to the continuing practice of religion in modern life.

17. _____ Religion is a part of all known cultures.

18. _____ The patriarchal nature of Western society is expressed in its theology.

19. _____ Shamanism is absent in modern industrial societies like the United States.

Answers to true/false practice questions

1. T	6. F	11. F	16. T
2. T	7. T	12. F	17. T
3. F	8. F	13. F	18. T
4. T	9. T	14. T	19. F
5. T	10. F	15. T	

Practice Matching

Match the culture with its characteristic.

1. _____Navajo

2. _____Tewa

3. _____Ibibio

4. _____Sioux

5. _____Mende

a. West African people who practice female initiation rite involving clitoridectomy.

b. Southwestern Native Americans with a witchcraft tradition.

c. Native Americans of the plains who started the Ghost Dance as a religious revitalization.

d. Native Americans of New Mexico whose origin myth reflects and validates their social structure.

e. Sub-Saharan African people with a witchcraft tradition.

Answers to practice matching

1. b   2. d   3. e   4. c   5. a

Practice Essays

1. Bronislaw Malinowski, in his classic essay *Magic, Science, and Religion*, claimed that each of these was a viable mode of cognition and that most societies exhibit all of them in variable proportions. In what ways does magical thinking persist in contemporary North America? Is it likely to persist into the future?

2. Identify and describe the various ways the Jo/'hoansi activate the powerful healing force called n/um.

3. How is modern medicine reconciled with traditional beliefs in Swaziland?

4. What is shamanism and how can the widespread occurrence of shamanism be explained?

5. Religious rituals are religion in action. Describe what in fact is accomplished by religious rituals.

6. What is a revitalization movement? Explain how an why do they come into existence?

Chapter 14
The Arts

Synopsis

Chapter 14 examines the ethnocentric assumptions implicit in most Western definitions of the arts and artists. It distinguishes different types of creative activity such as the verbal arts, music, and sculpture and attempts to come up with a cross-culturally valid definition of art.

What You Should Learn from This Chapter

1. Understand why anthropologists are interested in the arts.

2. Understand the forms of verbal arts and how they function in society:
   - myth
   - legend
   - tale

3. Understand the function of music.

4. Understand the range of visual and plastic arts in human societies.

Key Terms

construal

entopic phenomena

epic

ethnomusicology

folklore

folkloristics

iconic images

legend

motif

myth

tale

tonality

Review Questions

1. Distinguish between secular and religious art.

2. What are the basic kinds of verbal arts studied by anthropologists?

3. Give an example of how myth expresses the world view of a people.

4. Distinguish between legend and myth.

5. Why is matriarchy a common theme in many societies' myths?

6. What role does poetry play in the lives of the Bedouins?

7. What type of society is likely to have epics? Why?

8. What aspects of legends are of interest to anthropologists?

9. Why are anthropologists interested in tales?

10. What are the functions of music?

11. Distinguish between art and craft.

12. What is the importance of entopic phenomena?

13. What is the "second stage" of trance?

14. Are there any universal characteristics of art?

15. Why do marketing experts routinely employ music and pictorial images in their advertising?

Fill-in-the-Blank

1. The term "verbal arts" is preferred to the term _____, a term developed in the nineteenth century to refer to traditional oral stories of European peasants.

2. The word "myth," in _____ usage, refers to something that is widely believed to be true but isn't.

3. Tabaldak and Odziozo are characters in the origin myth of the _____.

4. Legends are _____ narratives that recount the deeds of heroes, the movements of people, and the establishment of customs.

5. Studies of tales in the southeast United States now indicate that they originated in _____ rather than Europe.

6. "Little songs" that occur every day were studied among the _____.

7. The study of music in its cultural setting is called _____.

8. The term _____ is used to refer to scale systems and their modifications in music.

9. An alternative to the Western octave system is the _____, which is defined by five equidistant tones.

10. Two people playing different patterns of beats at the same time is called
    _____.

11. The cultures of _____ have a particularly rich tradition of sculpture.

12. Among the Pomo Indians of California, _____ is an important
    expression of aesthetic interest.

13. The human nervous system produces images out of which patterns are construed.
    These are called _____.

Multiple-Choice Practice Questions

1. Whether useful or non-useful, all art is an expression of _____.
   a. the innate need to be impractical.
   b. a fundamental human capacity for religious expression.
   c. state-level societies that can afford specialists.
   d. political domination of minorities by elites.
   e. the symbolic representation of form and the expression of feeling that constitutes
      creativity.

2. The observation that all cultures include activities that provide aesthetic pleasure
   suggests that _____.
   a. humans may have an innate or acquired need to produce art.
   b. the human mind requires the stimulation of imaginative play to prevent boredom.
   c. all societies, from food-foraging bands to industrial states, include art in their
      culture.
   d. art is a necessary activity in which all normal, active members of society
      participate.
   e. all of the above

3. Anthropologists prefer to use the term *verbal arts* rather than the term *folklore*
   because the term _____.
   a. *folklore* is used only by linguists; the term *verbal arts* is used only by
      anthropologists.
   b. *verbal arts* sounds more sophisticated.
   c. *verbal arts* is more scientific.
   d. *folklore* implies lack of sophistication and is a condescending term to use.
   e. *folklore* refers only to fairy tales.

4. The type of verbal arts that has received the most study and attention is

   _____.
   a. poetry.
   b. incantations.
   c. narratives.
   d. proverbs.
   e. riddles.

5. In the myth of Tabaldak and Odziozo, Tabaldak first created the Abenakis from stone
   and then from living wood. What does this tell us about the functions of myth?
   a. Myths function to tell actual history; the Abenakis believe that they were
      originally made of wood.
   b. Myths bring humor into the lives of the Abenakis because the myths are so
      ridiculous.
   c. Myths function primarily to provide entertainment; the Abnakis know they were
      not made from wood, but like to tell this story to visiting anthropologists who are
      so gullible.
   d. Myths function to express a culture's world view; the Abenakis see themselves as
      belonging to the world of living things rather than to the nonliving world of stone.
   e. Myths provide skills of woodworking and stone masonry to the Abenakis.

6. Because legends contain details of a people's past, they are a form of history;
   because they often give a picture of a people's view of the world and humanity's
   place in it, they are like _____.
   a. poetry.
   b. religion.
   c. magic.
   d. kinship systems.
   e. myths.

7. When an anthropologist uses the term _____, he or she is referring to a
   category of verbal narratives that are secular, non-historical, and seen primarily as a
   source of entertainment.
   a. "folklore"
   b. "myth"
   c. "tale"
   d. "legend"
   e. "drama"

8. Your text describes a type of narrative found in many cultures in which a peasant father and his son, while traveling with their beast of burden, meet a number of people who criticize them. What is the motif?
   a. The "motif" refers to the psychological motives of the characters in a story, in this case the desire of the son to do better than his father.
   b. "Motif" means the historical background to the story, in this case the history of exploitation of the peasantry.
   c. The "motif" refers to the story situation, in this case a father and son trying to please everyone.
   d. "Motif" means the physical environment in which the story occurs, in this case the yam gardens of Ghana.
   e. The "motif" refers to the economic background, in this case feudalism.

9. The "little songs" of the Bedouin are considered un-Islamic; they are the discourse of children, used to express rebellious ideas and feelings. Thus they are _____.
   a. anti-structural.
   b. forbidden.
   c. sung among Europeans only.
   d. sung only when the Bedouins are away from their homeland.
   e. sung only at marriages.

10. The field of ethnomusicology _____.
   a. is concerned with human music rather than natural music.
   b. is the study of music in its cultural setting.
   c. began in the nineteenth century with the collection of folk songs.
   d. concerns the organization of melody, rhythm, and form in a culture's music.
   e. all of the above

11. Scale systems and their modifications in music are called _____.
   a. tonality.
   b. ethnomusicology.
   c. sculpture.
   d. verbal arts.
   e. pentatonic.

12. During the Washington Peace March in the sixties, thousands of people sang the song "We Shall Overcome." This song expressed a feeling of common purpose to counteract repression and to reform society. It created a sense of unity among diverse members of the crowd. This example illustrates the _____ of music.
    a. social functions
    b. geographical distribution
    c. tonality
    d. mythological features
    e. polyrhythms

13. Objects that are trivial, low in symbolic content, or impermanent are usually considered products of _____.
    a. an ethnomusicologist.
    b. a tale.
    c. craft.
    d. art.
    e. sculpture.

14. Amongst the Kalahari groups of the 1950s and 1960s, about half the men and a third of the women were _____.
    a. rock artists
    b. shaman
    c. hunters
    d. gatherers
    e. chiefs

15. For this group of Native Americans basketmaking has been important for their sense of who they are since before European contact.
    a. Cheyenne
    b. Hurok
    c. Pomo
    d. Chumash
    e. Comanche

16. After comprehensive archaeological, ethnographic, and other studies were completed in 1976, anthropologist _____ succeeded in having the Pomo basketry materials recognized by the National Register of Historic Places as "historic property."
    a. Richard N. Lerner
    b. Edward C. Green
    c. L. Abu-Lughod
    d. William L. Ury
    e. G. Koch

17. As the British anthropologist Raymond Firth observed: "_____ is an art of making sense out of experience, and like any other art, say, poetry, it must be taken symbolically, not literally."
    a. Entertainment
    b. Music
    c. Dance
    d. Religion
    e. Painting

18. In the United States numerous examples exist of marginalized social and ethnic groups attempting to gain a larger audience and more compassion for their plight through song. Perhaps no better example exists than _____.
    a. Mexican Americans.
    b. Chinese Americans.
    c. Native Americans.
    d. Puerto Ricans.
    e. African Americans.

19. A surprisingly large number of _____ in European and African tales are traceable to ancient sources in India.
    a. stories
    b. myths
    c. motifs
    d. devices
    e. lines

20. Which of the following music forms emerged out of the African American experience in the United States?
    a. opera
    b. polka
    c. ranchera
    d. waltz
    e. jazz

21. What do White performers like Elvis Presley and Pat Boone have in common?
    a. They were not influenced by African American music.
    b. They wrote their own music.
    c. They wrote their own lyrics.
    d. They presented their own versions of African American music to Black audiences.
    e. They presented their own versions of African American music to White audiences.

22. Perhaps the oldest form of artistic expression is _____.
    a. oil painting.
    b. sculpting.
    c. pottery.
    d. body decoration.
    e. cave drawings.

23. A true _____ is basically religious, in that it provides a rationale for religious beliefs and practices.
    a. folktale
    b. legend
    c. myth
    d. epic tale
    e. riddle

24. Much of what passes for history, consists of the _____ we develop to make ourselves feel better about who we are.
    a. poems
    b. parables
    c. legends
    d. ballads
    e. fictions

25. A surprisingly large number of motifs in European and African tales are traceable to ancient sources in _____.
    a. China.
    b. Japan.
    c. Latin America.
    d. India.
    e. Mesopotamia.

26. Applying the interpretive approach to southern African rock art requires knowledge of which two subjects?
    a. Mbuti ethnography
    b. Busman ethnography
    c. nature of the rain forest
    d. nature of the trance
    e. *b* and *d*

27. _____ serves as a powerful way for a social or ethnic group to assert its distinctive identity.
   a. Tales
   b. Music
   c. Chants
   d. Poems
   e. Plays

Answers to multiple-choice practice questions

1. e	8. c	15. c	22. d
2. e	9. a	16. a	23. c
3. d	10. e	17. d	24. c
4. c	11. a	18. e	25. d
5. d	12. a	19. c	26. e
6. e	13. c	20. e	27. b
7. c	14. b	21. e	

True/False Practice Questions

1. _____ The term "tale" refers to a type of narrative that is secular, non-historical, and seen primarily as a source of entertainment.

2. _____ Legends are semi-historical narratives which recount the deeds of heroes, the movement of peoples and the establishment of local customs.

3. _____ The word "myth," in popular usage, refers to something that is widely believed to be true but probably isn't.

4. _____ Legends provide clues as to what is considered appropriate behavior in a culture.

5. _____ Bushman rock images are banal, meaningless artifacts akin to urban graffiti in the U.S.

6. _____ Bushman art has a single, one-to-one 'meaning' that it unequivocally transmits from the maker to the viewer.

7. _____ Bushman rock art were simply records of religious experiences.

8. _____ Bushman rock art were not just pictures, but rather powerful things in themselves that could facilitate the mediation of the cosmological realms.

9. _____ Bushman rock art were just pictures that had no power to effect changes in the shamans' states of consciousness.

10. _____ The making of art was, for the Bushman, an idle pastime.

11. _____ For centuries shamans had fought in the spiritual realm with marauding shamans of illness, so, their art suggests, did they battle in the spiritual realm with the colonists.

12. _____ Bushman rock art itself and the belief system in which it was embedded is much more complex than was ever thought.

13. _____ As another organizing factor in music, whether regular or irregular, tonality may be more important than rhythm.

14. _____ The music of a marginalized group of former slaves eventually captivated the entire world, helping their descendants to escape their marginal status.

15. _____ In the United States, the arts often are seen as something of a frill, something to be engaged in for personal enjoyment apart from more productive pursuits or to provide pleasure for others, or both.

16. _____ A true myth is basically religious in that it provides a rationale for religious beliefs and practices.

17. _____ For the most part, legends and myths are the products solely of nonliterate, non-industralized societies.

Answers to true/false practice questions

1. T	6. F	11. T	16. T
2. T	7. F	12. T	17. F
3. T	8. T	13. F	
4. T	9. F	14. F	
5. F	10. F	15. T	

Practice Essays

1. Many famous biographies or novels about artists in the West stress the individual creativity of the artist (for example, James Joyce's *Portrait of the Artist as a Young Man*). Artists are portrayed as people who have the vision to rise above and beyond the social and cultural conditions into which they were born, sometimes even crossing the boundaries of normality as typically defined by society. How is this vision of the artist different from the conception of artists held by non-Western societies?

2. Discuss art's general meaning. What is art's role in Bushman communities?

3. Bushman rock art extends beyond the generation of religious experience to the negotiation of political power. Demonstrate why this is so.

4. Discuss why it is important to protect the cultural heritages of tribal peoples. Why is it of concern to anthropologists?

5. Discuss the influence the African American experience has had on American music.

6. What are the social functions of music? Provide examples.

Chapter 15
Cultural Change

Synopsis

Chapter 15 discusses the mechanisms of cultural change and examines anthropology's role in the changes sweeping the world. The use of the term "modernization" is considered from a cross-cultural perspective.

What You Should Learn from This Chapter

1. Understand how cultures change and the mechanisms involved:
   - innovation
   - diffusion
   - cultural loss
   - acculturation

2. Understand why the field of applied anthropology developed.

3. Understand how societies react to forcible change:
   - syncretism
   - revitalization movements

4. Understand the process of modernization and its effect on societies.

Key Terms and Names

acculturation

applied anthropology

diffusion

Franz Boas

genocide

integrative mechanism

modernization

nativistic (revivalistic) movement

primary innovation

revolutionary

secondary innovation

structural differentiation

syncretism

tradition

Review Questions

1. Distinguish between primary and secondary innovation.

2. Provide an example of primary innovation.

3. Why is it that cultural context provides the means for innovation to occur?

4. What things have European Americans borrowed from American Indians?

5. What is meant by cultural loss?

6. Describe the nature of acculturation.

7. What three factors seem to be underlying causes of genocide?

8. What does the field of applied anthropology attempt to accomplish?

9. How did the Trobriand Islanders react to the British game of cricket?

10. What is the purpose of revitalization movements?

11. What are the precipitators of rebellion and revolution?

12. What is the problem with the term "modernization"?

13. What are the four sub-processes of modernization?

14. What is meant by the "culture of discontent"?

Fill-in-the-Blank

1. Innovations based on the chance discovery of some new principle are called
   _____ innovations, while innovations resulting from the deliberate
   application of these principles are called _____ innovations.

2. The spread of customs or practices from one culture to another is called
   _____.

3. According to Ralph Linton, as much as _____ percent of a culture's
   content is due to borrowing.

4. _____ occurs when groups with different cultures come into intensive,
   firsthand contact and one or both groups experience massive cultural changes.

5. One society may retain its culture but lose its autonomy, becoming a
   _____ within the dominant culture.

6. The extermination of one people by another is called _____.

7. The field of _____ anthropology uses anthropological knowledge and
   techniques for practical purposes.

8. The applied work of anthropologist _____ helped reform the U.S.
   government's immigration policies.

9. Under conditions of acculturation, indigenous populations may blend foreign traits
   with those of their own culture to form a new cultural system. This response is called
   _____.

10. The Trobrianders blended indigenous traditions with the British game of
    _____.

11. _____ movements are deliberate attempts by members of a society to
    construct a more satisfactory culture.

12. A revitalization movement that attempts to bring back a destroyed but not forgotten
    way of life is called a _____ or revivalistic movement.

13. A revitalization movement that attempts to resurrect a suppressed, outcast group that
    has its own special subcultural ideology and has occupied an inferior social position
    for a long time is called _____.

14. Revolutions have occurred only during the last _____ years, since the emergence of centralized systems of political authority.

15. Modernization refers to the process of cultural and socioeconomic change whereby developing societies become more similar to _____ industrialized societies.

16. The _____ aspect of modernization means a shift in population from rural areas to cities.

17. The Skolt Lapps in the country of _____ traditionally supported themselves by fishing and reindeer herding.

18. The Shuar Indians promoted cooperative _____ ranching as their new economic base.

19. By the early 1970s the United States, encompassing 6 percent of the world's population, was consuming about _____ percent of the world's output of copper, coal, and oil.

20. The Wauja are a community of indigenous people whose claim to certain lands and the ceremonies that take place there are threatened by _____ and _____.

Exercise

Briefly identify and locate the following cultures.

1. Skolt Lapps

2. Shuar

3. Ju/'hoansi

4. Wauja

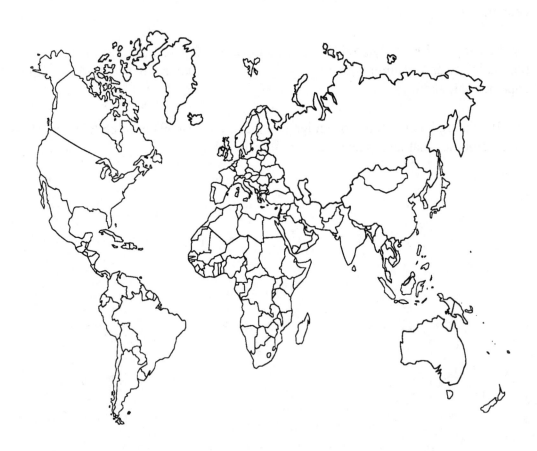

Multiple-Choice Practice Questions

1. In New England, the culture of English speakers replaced the various cultures of Native Americans living along the coast. Your text says that this occurred because _____.
   a. English-speaking culture was superior to Native American culture.
   b. Native American culture was superior to English-speaking culture.
   c. it is inevitable that English speakers will replace other cultures that they encounter.
   d. a combination of accidental factors contributed to the success of English speakers in establishing colonies along coastal New England.
   e. the success of English speakers was only a temporary setback for the progressive development of Native American culture.

2. The chance discovery of some new principle that can be applied in a variety of ways is called _____.
   a. primary innovation.
   b. primary syncretism.
   c. applied anthropology.
   d. millenarism.
   e. diffusion.

3. The deliberate use of basic ideas in some practical application, such as making use of the knowledge of how electricity works to develop the telephone, is called _____.
   a. revitalization.
   b. millenarism.
   c. modernization.
   d. integrative mechanism.
   e. secondary innovation.

4. Copernicus's discovery that the earth orbits the sun rather than vice versa _____.
   a. was a primary innovation that met the cultural goals and needs of his time.
   b. was a primary innovation that was out of step with the needs, values, and goals of the time.
   c. was a secondary innovation that put into application the discovery by Ptolemy that heavenly bodies moved on crystalline spheres around the earth.
   d. was a secondary innovation that was deliberately developed by Copernicus to destroy the Polish Church.
   e. resulted from diffusion of ideas from India.

5. According to the North American anthropologist Ralph Linton, about 90 percent of any culture's content comes from _____.
   a. primary innovation.
   b. diffusion.
   c. invention.
   d. syncretism.
   e. revolution.

6. In biblical times, chariots and carts were widespread in the Middle East, but by the sixth century the roads had deteriorated so much that wheeled vehicles were replaced by camels. This illustrates that cultural change is sometimes due to _____.
   a. primary invention.
   b. secondary invention.
   c. diffusion.
   d. revitalization.
   e. cultural loss.

7. As a result of prolonged firsthand contact between societies A and B, which of the following might happen?
   a. Society A might wipe out society B, with it becoming a new dominant society.
   b. Society A might retain its distinctive culture but lose its autonomy and come to survive as a subculture such as a caste or ethnic group.
   c. Society A might be wiped out by society B, with only a few scattered refugees living as members of the dominant society.
   d. The cultures of A and B might fuse, becoming a single culture with elements of both.
   e. all but *a*

8. The extermination of one group of people by another, often deliberately and in the name of progress, is called _____.
   a. genocide.
   b. acculturation.
   c. diffusion.
   d. applied anthropology.
   e. primary innovation.

9. The field of applied anthropology developed _____.
   a. through efforts to help the poor in North American society.
   b. in sociology classrooms.
   c. in industry.
   d. in colonial situations.
   e. through the efforts of women opposed to prohibition.

10. In acculturation, subordinate groups will often incorporate new cultural elements into their own culture, creating a blend of old and new; a reinterpretation of new cultural elements to fit them with already existing traditions is called _____.
    a. syncretism.
    b. innovation.
    c. diffusion.
    d. integrative mechanism.
    e. modernization.

11. A deliberate attempt by members of society to construct a more satisfying culture may be called _____.
    a. a secondary innovation.
    b. a revitalization movement.
    c. an enervating movement.
    d. syncretism.
    e. a primary innovation.

12. Which of the following is/are considered to be important precipitators of rebellion and revolution?
    a. A sudden reversal of recent economic advances.
    b. The media no longer support the government.
    c. The established leadership loses prestige.
    d. A strong, charismatic leader organizes attacks on the existing government.
    e. all of the above

13. The term "modernization" _____.
    a. is a relativistic rather than ethnocentric concept.
    b. refers to the process of cultural and socioeconomic change whereby societies acquire the characteristics of industrialized societies.
    c. refers to a global and all-encompassing process whereby modern cities gradually deteriorate.
    d. can be used to show that all societies go through the same stages of evolutionary development, culminating in the urban-industrial state.
    e. is not used by anthropologists.

14. As modernization occurs, which of the following changes are likely to follow?
    a. Literacy increases.
    b. Religion decreases.
    c. Kinship plays a less significant role.
    d. Social mobility increases.
    e. all of the above

15. The division of a single role (which serves several functions) into two or more roles (each with a single specialized function) is called _____.
   a. millenarization.
   b. modernization.
   c. structural differentiation.
   d. industrialization.
   e. diffusion.

16. Changes in Skolt Lapp society occurred because _____.
   a. men switched from reindeer herding to other sources of income.
   b. the number of reindeer declined.
   c. snowmobiles were used to herd reindeer.
   d. society became hierarchical.
   e. women became more powerful than men.

17. The indigenous people whom Pedro Alvares Cabral encountered in his "discovery" of Brazil in 1500.
   a. Yanomami
   b. Shuar
   c. Mekranoti
   d. Pataxo
   e. Inca

18. The Brazilian Indian service.
   a. BIA
   b. FOIRN
   c. NGOs
   d. FUNAI
   e. CIMI

19. _____ are street beggars that wander the streets in all major cities of Brazil.
   a. Fandango
   b. Pobres
   c. Mendingo
   d. Gente de las calles
   e. Gente sin casas

20. The most common pattern characterizing violence against indigenous people in Brazil is _____.
    a. racism.
    b. impunity (guilty party gets away with crime).
    c. massacres.
    d. illegal detention.
    e. police brutality.

21. When people are able to keep faith with their traditions in the face of powerful outside domination, the result is _____.
    a. depression.
    b. assimilation.
    c. cretinism.
    d. gratification.
    e. syncretism.

22. Over his career of 35 years of scholarly and applied work, _____, has made pioneering contributions to the development of applied anthropology and to anthropology's role in public policy and service.
    a. R.J. Gordon
    b. Michael M. Horowitz
    c. Pierre Van Den Berghe
    d. George Augustus Robinson
    e. August Dvorak

23. Horowitz's tireless dedication has been critical in institutionalizing anthropology as an applied science in international development organizations like which of the following?
    a. Nasdaq
    b. the World Bank
    c. USAID
    d. the Food and Agriculture Organization (FAO)
    e. all but *a*

24. The ultimate source of all change is _____.
    a. religion.
    b. war.
    c. innovation.
    d. the weather.
    e. biological.

25. _____ occurs when two cultures lose their separate identities and form a single culture, as expressed by the "melting pot" ideology of Anglo-American culture in the United States.
    a. Extinction
    b. Corruption
    c. Dissolution
    d. Synthesis
    e. Merger

26. In 1637 a deliberate attempt was made to destroy the Pequot Indians by setting fire to their village at Mystic, Connecticut and then shooting down all those who sought to escape being burned alive. This is considered an act of _____.
    a. attrition.
    b. contrition.
    c. absolution.
    d. genocide.
    e. fratricide.

27. In the present century, the scope of applied anthropology has broadened. Early on, the applied work of _____, considered by some to be the father of American anthropology, was instrumental in reforming U.S. immigration policies.
    a. Robert Lowie
    b. Napoleon Chagnon
    c. Walter Goldschmidt
    d. E. Adamson Hoebel
    e. Franz Boas

28. _____ movements that attempt to revive traditional ways of the past are not restricted to "underdeveloped" countries; in the U.S., the Reverend Pat Robertson is a leader in such a movement.
    a. New Age
    b. Mystical
    c. Revitalization
    d. Nostalgic
    e. Revolutionary

29. The process of modernization can be best understood as consisting of several subprocesses. Which of the following are subprocesses of modernization?
    a. extraterrestrial development
    b. technological development
    c. agricultural development
    d. weapons development
    e. *b* and *c*

30. Whereas most items for daily use were once made at home, such as butter, almost everything we use today is the product of specialized production, as is the butter we buy in the supermarket. This is a case of _____.
    a. urbanization.
    b. industrialization.
    c. structural differentiation.
    d. productive progress.
    e. efficient productivity.

31. The gap between the rich and poor people of the world is widening rather than narrowing. This has led to the development of what anthropologist Paul Magnarella has called a new _____.
    a. "culture of poverty."
    b. "culture of unrealized dreams."
    c. "culture of unrealistic expectations."
    d. "culture of discontent."
    e. "class of have nots."

Answers to multiple-choice practice questions

1. d	9. d	17. d	25. e
2. a	10. a	18. d	26. d
3. e	11. b	19. c	27. e
4. b	12. e	20. b	28. c
5. b	13. b	21. e	29. e
6. e	14. e	22. b	30. c
7. e	15. c	23. e	31. d
8. a	16. c	24. c	

True/False Practice

1. _____ In case after case, the scenario is revealed in which violent acts against Brazil's indigenous peoples are never brought to justice.

2. _____ In Brazil today, the judicial process in cases involving indigenous peoples has not gotten further than determining where the trial will be held.

3. _____ Brazil's indigenous peoples have shown that they are unable to resist or adapt to demands imposed upon them from outside.

4. _____ Brazilian society has shown that it is capable of overcoming two of its deepest internal conflicts: racism and the lack of punishment for those guilty of crimes against indigenous people (impunity).

5. _____ Brazil's indigenous peoples have shown that they are not merely "remnants" of a once great past, but are fully capable of forging viable models for their future.

6. _____ The impact of Michael M. Horowitz's applied anthropological research has been by all standards minimal.

7. _____ Acts of genocide are a fairly recent phenomena.

8. _____ Each revitalization movement that has occurred in the United States has been unique and different from the other.

9. _____ By their very nature, all revolts are revolutionary in their consequences.

10. _____ Haviland has made it quite clear that genocide is always a deliberate act.

11. _____ Because stability is a striking feature of many cultures like the food foragers, subsistence farmers, and pastoralists these cultures are changeless.

12. _____ Frequently, rather than just adding new things to those already in existence, the acceptance of a new innovation leads to the loss of an older one.

13. _____ Genocide is not always a deliberate act.

Answers to true/false practice questions

1. T	5. T	9. F	13. T
2. T	6. F	10. F	
3. F	7. F	11. F	
4. F	8. F	12. T	

Practice Matching

Match the culture with its characteristic.

1. _____ Skolt Lapps

2. _____ Shuar

3. _____ Wauja

4. _____ Iranians

5. _____ Tasmanians

a. Established an Islamic government after a successful religious revitalization.

b. An Amazonian people who mobilized to protect their native lands.

c. Native Americans of Ecuador who formed a federation to protect their interests.

d. Arctic Scandinavians whose society was radically changed by the introduction of snowmobiles.

e. Indigenous people off the coast of Australia who were wiped out by Europeans.

Answers to practice matching

1. d   2. c   3. b   4. a   5. e

Practice Essays

1. Describe the impact of modernization on Skolt Lapps, Shuar Indians, and Wauja.

2. In what ways can the rising tide of Islamic fundamentalism in the Middle East and other areas of the world be seen as a revitalization movement? Are there other terms from the chapter that could apply to this phenomenon? What might anthropology contribute to our understanding of such movements?

3. The violence that occurred on Indian Day in Brazil 1997 brought to the surface old problems and wounds that have never healed. Identify and discuss these old problems and wounds that still exist in Brazilian society.

4. Statistics gathered by the Indigenous Missionary Council show that not only is there an increase in violence against Brazil's indigenous people, but also in the kinds of aggression committed against them. Identify the new forms of aggression against the indigenous peoples of Brazil. How are these cases represented and reported in the national press and how are they dealt with by authorities? Are there patterns in the violence that characterize Indian/white relations?

5. Explain why revolution is a relatively recent phenomena.

6. Discuss the contributions of Michael M. Horowitz to the development of applied anthropology and to anthropology's role in public policy and service.

7. Reactions of indigenous peoples to changes forced upon them vary considerably. Describe how various groups have reacted to forced change.

8. Belief in "progress" and its inevitability has important implications for North Americans as well as others. What are the implication? Explain.

Chapter 16
The Future of Humanity

Synopsis

In this concluding chapter the text considers the role of anthropological knowledge in facing the world of the future.

What You Should Learn from This Chapter

1. Understand the contribution anthropology can make in planning for humanity's future.

2. Understand what a one-world culture is and the feasibility of such a system.

3. Consider the problems facing humankind and some possible avenues of solution.

Key Terms

cultural pluralism

"culture of discontent"

ethnic resurgence

global apartheid

one-world culture

replacement reproduction

structural violence

Review Questions

1. What shortcomings are evident in future-oriented literature?

2. What makes anthropologists uniquely suited to contribute to planning for the future?

3. Can the globe today be described as a "one-world culture"?

4. Why are predictions of a politically integrated world probably incorrect?

5. Give an example of how misunderstandings might actually increase in a one-world culture.

6. Give some contemporary examples of ethnic resurgence.

7. How does the concept of ethnocentrism interfere with cultural pluralism?

8. In what way is the world system one of "global apartheid"?

9. Provide examples of structural violence.

10. What is thought to be the immediate cause of world hunger? Provide examples.

11. Why is the suggestion that countries adopt agricultural practices similar to the United States not necessarily sound advice?

12. What is meant by the "exploitative world view"?

Fill-in-the-Blank

1. Anthropologists try to be _____, meaning they take into account many interacting factors to understand the functioning of the complex whole.

2. Anthropologists have a _____, meaning they take a long-term view of things.

3. Over the past five thousand years, political units have grown steadily _____ in size and _____ in number.

4. All large states have a tendency to _____.

5. There are about _____ recognized states in the world today, but an estimated 5,000 national groups.

6. An important force for global unity are the _____ corporations that cut across national boundaries.

7. The separation of whites and blacks in South Africa under the domination of the white minority was a system called _____.

8. About _____ of the population of the world is nonwhite.

9. A great deal of the violence in the world is not due to the unique and personal decisions of individuals but to social, political, and economic conditions; this is referred to as _____ violence.

10. The population of the world today is about _____.

11. The cause of world hunger is not so much the ability to produce food but the ability to _____ it effectively.

12. _____ rain, caused in part by smokestack gases, is causing damage to lakes, forests, and ground water.

13. All civilizations have an _____ world view that tends to promote ecologically unsound cultural practices.

14. Replacement reproduction refers to a rate of reproduction in which a couple have no more than _____ children.

Multiple-Choice Practice Questions

1. Most people plan for the future by looking at trends in _____.
   a. ancient history.
   b. hemlines.
   c. third-world countries.
   d. food supplies.
   e. recent history.

2. Anthropologists are trained to develop effective predictions of the future because they are _____.
   a. aware of cultural relativity.
   b. good at seeing how parts fit together into a large whole.
   c. trained to have an evolutionary perspective.
   d. able to see short-term trends in long-term perspective.
   e. all of the above

3. Over the past five thousand years, political units have _____.
   a. grown steadily smaller in size.
   b. grown steadily larger in size and fewer in number.
   c. eliminated multinational corporations.
   d. promoted individual freedoms.
   e. eliminated slavery.

4. Multinational corporations _____.
   a. have been widespread in Western culture since medieval times.
   b. were very common during the colonial period.
   c. have become a major force in the world today since the 1950s.
   d. have been disintegrating since the 1950s.
   e. promote relativistic rather than ethnocentric ideas.

5. Which of the following expresses the **negative** consequences of multinational corporations on the international and domestic scenes?
   a. Multinational corporations cross-cut nations and thus achieve a global unity.
   b. Multinational corporations have become a major force in the world since the 1950s.
   c. Multinational corporations have become so powerful that they have been able to influence government decisions so that they benefit the company rather than the people.
   d. Multinational corporations are products of the technological revolution.
   e. They have developed sophisticated data-processing techniques that enable them to keep track of worldwide operations.

6. Cultural pluralism _____.
   a. may constitute a temporary stage in a process of integration into a single melting-pot culture.
   b. implies the absence of bigotry and racism.
   c. implies respect for the cultural traditions of other peoples.
   d. may result from conquest or from several culturally distinct groups occupying an area that eventually becomes unified as a larger political entity.
   e. all of the above

7. Which of the following represent the **negative** consequences of ethnocentrism?
   a. By believing that another culture is inferior to yours, you can, with a sense of righteousness, destroy its temples, cottage industry, polygynous practices, and so on in order to bring it into line with your culture's standards of appropriate behavior and belief.
   b. Ethnocentrism confers a sense of pride in and loyalty to one's own cultural traditions.
   c. Ethnocentrism provides a feeling of psychological gratification that one is living the right kind of life.
   d. Ethnocentrism contributes to a sense of personal worth.
   e. Ethnocentrism strengthens social solidarity.

8. "Global apartheid" refers to _____.
   a. the prediction that in the future, South Africa will dominate the world economy.
   b. the fact that whites, although they make up only one-third of the world's population today, have greater access to the world's resources.
   c. the fact that nonwhites suffer a disproportionate share of the world's problems of hunger, pollution, and overpopulation and have a much greater chance of dying a violent death than do whites.
   d. the fact that the structure of world society is very similar to that of South Africa.
   e. all of the above except *a*

9. _____ is violence produced by social, political, and economic structures rather than by the unique and personal decisions of individuals.
   a. Torture
   b. Modernization
   c. Structural violence
   d. Insanity
   e. Religion

10. The change from subsistence farming to cash crops _____.
    a. enables farmers to enlarge their holdings and feed their families more effectively.
    b. results in the relocation of subsistence farmers to urban areas or to lands ecologically unfit for farming.
    c. leads to the decline of multinational corporations.
    d. supports cultural pluralism.
    e. leads to revitalization.

11. The main reason an Asian wet-rice farmer might choose not to adopt North American techniques of intensive agriculture is because _____.
    a. he or she cannot afford to buy the chemical products typically used in this type of agriculture.
    b. the North American method requires at least eight calories of energy to be expended for every calorie produced, whereas the wet-rice farmer produces three hundred calories for every calorie he or she invests.
    c. the North American method produces toxic substances that destroy delicate ecological balances.
    d. he or she predicts that the North American method, while successful for a short period of time, is sowing the seeds of its own destruction.
    e. all of the above

12. Pollution, although a worldwide consequence of certain agricultural and industrial activities, is more of a problem in _____ because chemicals that may be banned in richer nations can be used more easily.
    a. poor countries
    b. industrialized countries
    c. arctic countries
    d. Mediterranean countries
    e. ocean areas

13. If a country achieves "replacement reproduction," this means that _____.
    a. people produce only enough children to replace themselves when they die.
    b. each reproductive couple has no more children.
    c. its population will immediately stop growing.
    d. its population will continue to grow for another fifty years.
    e. every other generation can have children.

14. The most extreme form of female genital mutilation.
    a. female circumcision
    b. breast implantation
    c. infibulation
    d. appendectomy
    e. tonsillectomy

15. The most dramatic illustrations of the tendency for states to come apart recently would be which of the following?
    a. The breakup of the Soviet Union.
    b. The breakup of Yugoslavia.
    c. The separation of East Timor from Indonesia.
    d. The separation of Vietnam into North and South Vietnam.
    e. *a, b,* and *c*

16. The dramatic revival of pastoral nomadism in Mongolia would be an example of _____.
    a. cultural pluralism.
    b. cultural decline.
    c. nationalistic pride.
    d. ethnic backwardness.
    e. resistance to modernization.

17. Presently in the world, the _____ richest individuals have a combined wealth equal to the annual income of the poorest 47 percent of the entire world's population.
    a. 125
    b. 225
    c. 350
    d. 472
    e. 555

18. The immediate cause of world hunger has more to do with which of the following?
    a. food production
    b. food distribution
    c. food storage
    d. warfare
    e. *b* and *d*

19. The world's population is projected to peak in 49 years at about _____ billion people.
    a. 20
    b. 7.5
    c. 9.37
    d. 8.35
    e. 5.23

20. Which of the following would make the anthropologist well-equipped to make valid projections about the world's future?
    a. their holistic perspective
    b. their evolutionary perspective
    c. their 100 years of cross-cultural research
    d. their familiarity with alternative ways to deal with a wide variety of problems
    e. all of the above

21. Which of the following groups of women experience body mutilation as part of engendering rites?
    a. North American
    b. Sudanese
    c. Filipino
    d. Mexican
    e. *a* and *b*

22. After a 10-year intensive study of relations between producers and consumers of products and services, anthropologist _____ found repeated and documented offenses by business that cannot be handled by present complaint mechanisms, either in or out of court.
    a. Margaret Mead
    b. Laura Nader
    c. Ruth Benedict
    d. Linda Coco
    e. Howard Zinn

23. Sometimes, resistance to modernization takes the form of a _____ reaction, as it did in Iran and as is happening today in Algeria.
    a. revivalistic
    b. rebellious
    c. fundamentalist
    d. pluralistic
    e. allergic

24. The problem with _____ is that it all too easily can be taken as a charter for manipulating other cultures for the benefit of one's own, even though this does not have to be the choice.
    a. ethnocentrism
    b. ambivalence
    c. provincialism
    d. prejudice
    e. narrow-mindedness

25. Which of the following are reasons impoverished people tend to have so many children?
    a. Children are their main resource.
    b. Children provide a needed labor pool to work farms.
    c. Children are the only source of security for the elderly.
    d. Infant mortality rates are unusually high in impoverished areas.
    e. all of the above

26. In order to solve the problems brought about by global structural violence it has been suggested that dramatic changes in cultural values and motivations, as well as social institutions, will be required. Which of the following would have to change to help solve the problems due to structural violence?
    a. the emphasis on individual self-interest
    b. uncontrolled materialism
    c. a sense of social responsibility
    d. excessive consumption
    e. all but *c*

27. However humanity changes biologically, _____ remains the chief means by which humans try to solve their problems.
    a. technology
    b. religion
    c. faith in humankind
    d. military might
    e. culture

Answers to multiple choice practice questions

1. e	8. e	15. e	22. b
2. e	9. c	16. e	23. c
3. b	10. b	17. b	24. a
4. c	11. a	18. e	25. e
5. c	12. a	19. c	26. e
6. e	13. a	20. e	27. e
7. a	14. c	21. e	

True/False Practice Questions

1. _____ Multinational corporations have constituted a strong force for global unity.

2. _____ Structural violence refers to violence produced by social, political, and economic structures rather than by the unique and personal decisions of individuals.

3. _____ The change from subsistence farming to cash crops leads to economic improvements in countries that made the change.

4. _____ Modernization refers to a situation in which groups with different ways of acting and thinking can interact socially with mutual respect.

5. _____ The question of choice is central to the story of how medicine and business generate controlling processes in the shaping of women's bodies.

6. _____ Sudanese and other African women, North American women, and others experience body mutilation as part of engendering rites.

7. _____ The American Society of Plastic and Reconstructive Surgery operates like a commercial enterprise instead of a medical society. They saturate the media to sell women breast implants. The author of the original study, Linda Coco, refers to this idea as "patriarchal capitalism."

8. _____ Social surveys indicate that, to the extent that women internalize the social imperative that they can enhance their lives by enhancing their breasts, they feel they are making the decision on their own.

9. _____ In the Sudan, the young girl is told that circumcision and infibulation are done to her not for her.

10. _____ According to Linda Coco, the operation on the female breast in North America does **not** hold the same symbolism and expression of cultural mandate as does infibulation in Sudan.

11. _____ The interest of Cultural Survival, Inc. is to preserve indigenous cultures in their original pristine condition so that they will be there to study and to serve as living museum exhibits.

12. _____ Much remains to be done to secure the survival of indigenous peoples in all parts of the world.

13. _____ The Native American attempts to secure greater political sovereignty is an indication that the United States is not immune to breakup.

14. _____ In Guatemala robberies, assaults, torture, and death threats against human rights groups, journalists, and nongovernmental organizations were on the increase in the year 2000.

15. _____ According to Haviland's textbook, most of the world's weapons of mass destruction are owned by whites.

16. _____ The immediate cause of world hunger has less to do with warfare than with food production and food distribution.

17. _____ Multinationals are an extremely new phenomena on the global scene, appearing first around the 1950s.

18. _____ According to the original study "Standardizing the Body," the question of choice is central to the story of how medicine and business generate controlling processes in the shaping of women's bodies.

19. _____ In so-called "underdeveloped" countries, women have become a source of cheap labor for large corporations, as subsistence farming has given way to mechanized farming.

20. _____ It seems the more divergent cultural traditions are, the easier it is to make pluralism work.

21. _____ Though a minority of the world's population, people in the developed countries consume the most resources and generate the bulk of hazardous wastes.

Answers to true/false practice questions

1. T	7. T	13. T	19. T
2. T	8. T	14. T	20. F
3. F	9. F	15. T	21. T
4. F	10. F	16. F	
5. T	11. F	17. F	
6. T	12. T	18. T	

Practice Essays

1. The effort to reduce population growth faces enormous cultural obstacles. Illustrate this by describing Chinese efforts to promote one-child families, and consider whether Western planners should attempt to encourage similar efforts in the Islamic world, where birth control is prohibited on religious grounds. Where does appropriate global planning run up against the charge of ethnocentrism or cultural imperialism?

2. One of the most heated debates arising from the public health concern over breast implants is whether the recipient's decision is voluntary or whether control is disguised as free will. Explain what is meant by this.

3. What is the main interest of the advocacy group Cultural Survival, Inc.? Describe what they are trying to do for indigenous peoples. What are some of their success stories?

4. Despite a worldwide trend toward "Westernization," and despite the pressure for traditional cultures to disappear, it is clear that cultural differences are still very much with us in the world today. In fact, a tendency for peoples globally to resist modernization, and in some cases retreat from it, is strengthening. How can this be? Explain, using examples.

5. Discuss the rise of multinational corporations and their impact on the domestic as well as the international scene.

6. Debate the pros and cons of a "one-world culture."

7. Identify and discuss the problems of structural violence.

8. Solving the problems of the global society depends on, among other things, lessening the gap between the living standards of the impoverished and developed countries. How can this be accomplished?